Community Küche (Kitchen) Haus in West Amana

This West Amana Küche was build in 1850's. I was born in this Haus. It was my duty at the age of 14 to learn to cook from my mother who was The Küche Boss. We served 30-40 People a day.

I worked in the Küche 2 years, before the Change in 1932.

Painting 1987

With God, all things are possible.
Why pause or hesitate?
If there are things you want to do,
Why sit around and wait?
Small miracles are happening
about you every day,
With God, all things are possible...
Just bow your head and pray!

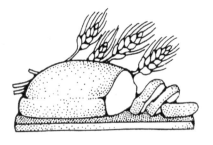

Acknowledgement
& Dedications

To the person who established my roots in Amana in German cooking my mother Lina Graesser, she was only a great cook & good teacher, she was the West Amana Kitchen Bosse. Her method, of cooking were taught to her at an early age.

To the person whose sweet tooth influenced the art of intricate baking my mother-in-law Henrietta Selzer.

In continuing with tradition it is with lots of love that I dedicate this book to my children.

Lial & Helen Selzer

Marian & Dan Carew

My grand children

Alisa - Dougie Hartman

Stephanie - Neal Vasso

Neil - Rebecca Selzer

Scott Selzer

For if it were not for their continued recipe requests, the inspiration for this book would not have happened.

What started out to be a make-shift file system, became a full-fled cook book with their encouragement.

Linda Selzer

Special garden

First, plant five rows of peas:
preparedness, promptness,
perseverance, politeness &
prayer.
Next to them, plant three rows
of squash:
criticism & squash indifference
Then five rows of lettuce:
let us be faithful,
let us be unselfish,
let us be loyal,
let us be truthful,
let us love one another & no
garden is complete without
turnips:
Turn up for church,
turn up with a smile.
Turn up with Determination

II

Recipe for a Happy Family

1-husband and Children
1-wife
1-Bible for each
1-Home
3-cups love (firmly packed)
1-package work
1- " playing together
1-portion patience
1- " understanding
1- " forgiveness
1-small paddle
1-cup of kisses
& generous portions of prayer.

Love is the ribbon that weaves two hearts together.

Old Time Gingerbread
Found in a real old cook book

I always take some flour – just enough for the cake I want to make.

I mix it up with some buttermilk if I happen to have some of it, just enough for the flour. Then I take some ginger, some like more, some like less, I put in a little salt & pearl ash, then I tell one of my children to pour in blops of molasses, til I tell him to stop. Then the children bring in wood to build up a good fire, & then we have gingerbread for company.

Contents

Brennan Printing
702 Locust St.
Deep River, Iowa 52222
1-800-448-3740

Appetizers...

Giant Taco Dip

Spread in layers:
2 - cans refried beans
1 - 6oz. can avocado dip
1 - 6oz.   "   jalapeno
1 - sm.   "   taco sauce

Sprinkle with:
Chopped green Olives
      "   black   "
1. can green chili
   chopped green onions
1 - cup shredded cheddar Cheese
decorate with cherry tomatoes

Serve with Nachos

Meat Balls "The best"

Combine -

1-lb. ground lean beef
1-lb.   "   pork sausage
1-cup bread crumbs
2-eggs -dash pepper
2-T. soy sauce
½-t. garlic salt
⅓-cup catsup
2-T. minced onions

mix- form into balls, size of a walnut, place on cookie sheet.
Bake 350° turning them until brown.

Sauce -

Combine and stir until smooth.

1-T. lemon juice
1-12oz. bottle Chili Sauce
1-can jellied Cranberries

Arrange meat balls in casserole and pour sauce over.
store in refrigerator over night
          Bake 350° 35-40 mins.
Very good appetizers.

Lord, let us reach out and give of ourselves to help others. Amen.

4

Gourmet Shrimp Spread

1 - 8 oz. pkg. soft Cream Cheese
2 - 4½ oz. can tiny shrimp, rinsed & drained
2 - T. lemon juice
¼ - cup mayonnaise
1 - T. chopped fresh parsley
½ - t. dill weed

Combine all ingredients. At medium
speed, until well mixed.
Remove to serving dish, cover, chill-
until ready to serve.

yield - 2 cups

Cheese Ball

1 - 8 oz. cream cheese
¾ - lb. Cheddar ..
1 - onion - minced
1 - T. liquid smoke or more
1 - t. garlic powder
¼ - cup chopped pecans

Soften cheese. mix all ingredients
well, shape into 2 balls.

Roll in chopped pecans. can also use
bacon bits.

Crab & Chili Sauce Pie

1 - 8 oz. Cream Cheese
1 - T. horseradish
2 - T. mayonnaise
1 - small onion - finely chopped
1 - bottle chili sauce
2 - 6 oz. cans flaked crab meat
 can use imitation crab.

Blend cheese, horseradish, mayonnaise,
Onions, spread on plate - store in
refrigerator over night.

Spread chili sauce over top, flake crab
meat on top. Sprinkle with fresh chopped
parsley.

Serve with toast or crackers

Best Stuffed Mushrooms

1. lb. large mushrooms - 20 - 25
1. T. butter
1. T. chopped fine onions
1. T. dry bread crumbs
1. 4¾ oz. Chunky Chicken spread
2. t. prepared mustard
1. t. Worcestershire sauce

Stem mushrooms, soak in boiling-water for 5 mins. Chop stems, cook in butter & onions until tender, add bread crumbs, chicken spread, mustard and worcestershire sauce.

Drain caps & spread on a foil lined-cookie sheet, fill caps with mixture & broil until lightly browned.
Serve warm.
Can make ahead & put under broiler, just as guests arrive.

Smoky Salmon Ball

1- 16oz. can red salmon drained
skin and bone removed
1- 8oz. Cream Cheese
1- medium onion grated
1- t. pickle relish, drained
1- t. liquid smoke
1- t. lemon juice
½- cup chopped walnuts.

Combine first 6 ingredients, mix thoroughly. Place on plastic wrap, form into balls (2) cover v chill.

Before serving roll in chopped walnuts.

Life is alot like tennis - the goal is to learn to serve best.

Potato Skins

6 - medium potatoes
1 - lb. ground beef
1 - medium onion chopped
1 - t. salt + 1/2 - t. pepper
1 - pkg. taco seasoning
1 - 12 oz. pkg. fine shredded mozzarelle cheese
1 - 12 oz " Cheddar cheese
chives, bacon bits, + sour cream

Brown beef, onions, add salt + pepper.
Drain grease, add taco seasoning + simmer
for 5 minutes.
Bake potatoes at 425°. 1 hour or until done
cut in half lengthwise, scoop out center,
leaving 1/4 inch around edges.
Sprinkle potatoes with cheddar cheese.
add 2 T. of beef mixture top with
mozzarella cheese.
Sprinkle with chives + bacon bits - heat
until cheese is melted.
Serve with sour cream.

Lobster Balls

1. cup cooked Lobster meat
1 - 3oz. pkg. Cream Cheese
1 - t. lemon juice
½ - t. celery seed
½ - t. salt - dash pepper

Combine all ingredients, blend - well, chill. Shape into ¾" balls, stick a pretzel stick into each ball, just - before serving to serve as a handle.

Makes about 2 dozen.

Celery Pin Wheels

Separate stalks from 1 bunch celery
Fill each stalk with nippy spreading cheese. Put stalks back together; tie firmly ~ chill.
Slice crosswise ¼ - ½" thick

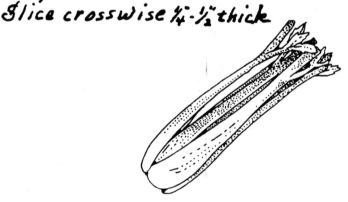

Cheese Crisp

Warm large flour tortilla under-broiler. Using pastry brush, spread tortilla lightly with melted butter. Sprinkle generously with grated longhorn Cheddar cheese. Place under broiler until cheese melts.

This easy hot appetizer may be topped with chopped green onions, chopped tomatoes, diced green chilies or cooked sausages – to become the

"Mexican pizza."

Copper Pennies

5- cups sliced carrots
Boil, not too soft - drain
1 - cup green peppers - sliced
1 -   "   Onions - sliced

Let come to a boil.
1 - can tomato soup
¼ - Cup Salad oil
¾ -   "   white vinegar
⅓ -   "   sugar
1 - t. worcestershire sauce
1 - t. salad mustard

Layer carrots, Onions, & peppers in disk, pour boiled ingredients over veggies

Store in Refrigerater.

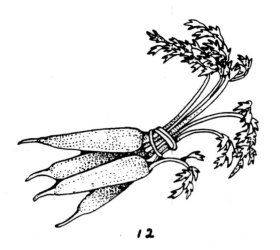

Broccoli roll ups

1-Loaf frozen bread dough
1- 10 oz. pkg. frozen broccoli
1-cup shredded cheese
2-T. chopped onions
1-egg
2-T. melted margarine
1-cup diced ham, chicken, or turkey

Roll out dough - 12 x 15 in. size

Combine all ingredients except margarine - spread on dough, roll up pinch to seal. Slice 1" pieces place on greased cookie sheet, & brush with melted margarine.

Bake 375° 20-25 mins
Good!

Many receive advice, only the wise profit by it.

13

Spinch Balls

1 - 10 oz. pkg. Frozen Spinach
1 - cup herbed stuffing mix
½ - " parmesan cheese
3 - eggs - beaten
6 - T. butter - softened

Cook spinach, ~ drain well, squeeze out juice.
Combine all ingredients ~ mix well.
(Can put in food processor)

Drop by t. on cookie sheet ~ freeze.

Take from freezer to oven.

Bake 350° - 10 mins
Serve hot.

Recipe from
Erna Wendler

Lord, thankyou for the many blessings that you have brought into our lives. Amen.

14

Cucumber Canapes

1 - 4 oz. Cream Cheese - soft
1 - pkg. dry Italian salad mix
2 - Lg. cucumbers - peeled & sliced
Dill weed
1 - loaf party rye bread

Mix cream cheese & italian salad mix
spread on rye bread - top with 1 slice
cucumber, sprinkle with dill weed.

Pickled Ham

1 - cup vinegar
1 - " water
1 - medium onion sliced
1½ - lbs. cooked ham
Cut ham into bite size cubes.
Mix vinegar & water
Combine ham & onions - fill in jar - pour
vinegar mixture over - close lid tight.
Refrigerate for 3-4 days.

Serve cold - always refrigerate.

Ham Spread

1 - 8 oz. pkg. Cream Cheese
¼ - cup mayonnaise
2 - cups ground ham
1 - T. parsley
1 - T. fine chopped onions
¼ - t. dry mustard

Blend all ingredients together
    Serve with crackers.

Cold Cut Roll-ups

Honey ham, cooked ham, or corned beef or
any meat slices.
Cheese spread – Kosher pickle spears.

Spread your favorite cheese spread on the
surface of a cold cut slice, top with a Kosher
pickle, roll up & chill
            Cut into 1" - pieces to serve.

Soup and Sandwiches

Barley Soup   19
Gourmet Cream of Zucchini Soup   20
Hearty Hamburger Soup   21
Clam Chowder   22
Taco Soup   23
No Fuss Cauliflower Soup   24
Meat Ball Vegetable Soup   25
Oma's Potato Soup   26
Black Bean Soup   27
Chicken Soup   28
Diet Soup   29

Grilled Sandwiches   30
Dutch Oven Sandwiches   31
Pizza Sandwiches   32
Delicious Chicken Spread   33
Alligator Stew   34

Barley Soup

3 - T. margarine - 2 - cloves garlic c.fine
3 - medium Onions - chopped fine
¾ - cup barley
8 - cups water
1 - cup celery - chopped fine
1 - " carrots - " "
½ - " peas
½ - " green beans
1 - small can corn

Saute -
Onions in margarine, add garlic.
water & rest of ingredients. add
5-7 t. chicken bouillon granules bring
to boil - reduce heat, cover & simmer
about 1 hour, until barley & vegetables
are tender.

10 - 1. cup servings

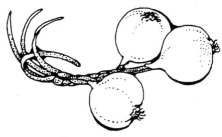

Lord, thank you for helping us learn
right from wrong. Amen.

Gourmet Cream of Zucchini Soup

4 - medium zucchini - sliced
3 - Cups onions - sliced
3 - T. margarine
4.5 cloves garlic
1 - cup parsley - fresh
5-6 t. chicken bouillon
6-8 cups of water
dash of pepper

In a large kettle saute onions in margarine till transparent. add rest ingredients. Cook until tender - cool - run thru blender.

Terrific with home made cubed bread, fried in margarine until crusty.

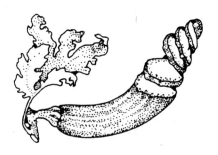

We may give without loving, but we cannot love without giving.

Hearty Hamburger Soup

1 - lb. ground beef
3 - medium onions, sliced
3 -   "   carrots   "
3 -   " stalks celery "
¼ - cup water
7 - cups   "
1 - 16 oz can stewed tomatoes
½ - cup quick cooking barley
¼ - "   "   "   rice
1 T. instant beef bouillon
1 T. salt 1 t monosodium glutamate

1- crumble beef in 1½-qt. casserole, cook in Radarange full Power 3-4 mins - stir half way through cooking time. Drain.

2- combine onions, carrots, celery & ¼ cup water in 4-qt. casserole. cook full-power. 12 mins. or until vegetable are tender. Stir halfway through cooking time

3- mix remaining ingredients. Cook covered on full Power or until. temperature of 160°F is reached - (30-35 mins.) let stand, covered 5 mins. before serving.

micro-Tip: use the Temperature-Control to stop Radarange oven at 160°s

21

Clam Chowder

2 - T. margarine
½ - cup diced onions ⎫ saute
4 - " " celery ⎭
1. bottle Clam juice
1. diced potato
2 - t. Chicken bouillon

Cook all till tender

add -
1 - can minced Clams
⅔ - cup carnation milk (1 can)
salt and pepper to taste.
Pinch of parsley.

Lord, thank you for touching us
with your love, guidance - healing.
                                Amen.

Taco Soup

½ - lb. ground beef
1 - medium onion -chopped
1 - large can tomatoes
1 - can whole kernel corn
1 - " kidney beans
2 - cups water
2 - T. taco mix
¼ - t. garlic salt
1 - t. seasoned salt

Brown beef, onions & put in soup pot.
add remaining ingredients. Bring
to a boil, simmer for 15-20 minutes.
This is very good when topped with
grated cheese, crumbled tortilla
chips and a dollop of sour cream.

Beauty is a gift.
    Charm must be cultivated

No Fuss Cauliflower Soup

2-cups chopped cauliflower
2- .. milk
2- T. margarine
2- t. chicken bouillon (granules)
1- t. minced onions
½- t. garlic powder
¼- t. celery salt
1-2-t. finely snipped parsley
½- cup instant potato flakes.

Heat milk, margarine, onions
chicken b., garlic & parsley just to
boiling - stir in potato flakes &
cooked cauliflower, heat 3-5 mins.
do not boil.
                    Sprinkle with parsley.
                         2-servings

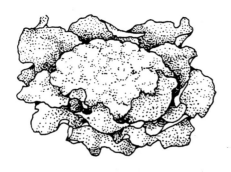

Lord, thank you for your everlasting
presence & Love.   Amen.

Meat Ball Vegetable Soup

Meat Balls:
1½-lb. ground beef
1-egg - ¼ t. salt
3-T. water
2-T. butter - 1. T. parsley
¼-cup bread crumbs
mix - make into meat balls brown
in oven.

In a large kettle, combine -
2-cups water
4-beef cubes
1-can tomatoes in juice
1½-cup chopped celery
1½- "   " onions
1½- "   " carrots
¼ - t. oregano
⅛ - t. pepper
4 - bay leaves
2-3 t. sugar
1-T. sweet basil
2- potatoes diced
1- can tomato sauce
1- can green beans

BASIL

Cook all for about 1 hour or until
Veggies are tender
                    Scott Selzer

25

Oma's - Potato Soup

- 3 - large potatoes - sliced thin
- 4 - slices lean bacon - diced
- 6 - flat leaves leek - sliced thin - chopped
- 1/4 - cup chopped onions
- 2 - T. flour
- 4 - cups chicken broth
- 2 - egg yolks - beaten
- 1 - cup sour cream
- 1 - T. chopped parsley
- 2 - T.   "   chervil

Saute bacon in a deep sauce pan 5 mins
add leek, onions, saute 5 mins, then stir
in flour ~ chicken broth, stirring constantly
add potatoes ~ simmer 1-hour. Combine
egg yolks ~ sour cream, stir that into soup.
simmer for 10 mins stirring constantly.
Add parsley ~ chervil. Serve with croutons.
　　　　makes about 2 quarts

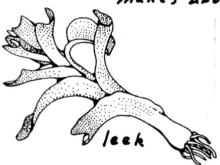

leek

Prayer is the key of the morning
and the bolt of the night.

Black - Bean - Soup

2 - cups black beans
8. " cold water
3. medium Onions - chopped
1/4. cup butter or margarine
2 - bay leaves
1 - large clove garlic - crushed
2 - T. parsley
1 - Ham hock
2/3 - cup dry sherry
    salt & pepper to taste

Soak beans overnite - drain, saute
onions, garlic, parsley in butter, add
8 cups water & beans - all ingredients
except sherry.
Cook 2-3 hrs. add more water if too thick.

Remove ham hock & cut in small pieces.
Can serve with shredded cheese or
chopped onions.
                    Makes 8 servings

            Kitchen of Marian Carew.

Prayer is the supersonic vehicle by
which we travel to God.

Chicken Soup

Cook 1 - 3-4 lb chicken
6 - cups water
2 - stalks celery
1 - onion sliced
2 - carrots cut in half
Salt & pepper to taste

Bring to boil - simmer until meat is
tender - about 1 hour. Strain broth -
use for the soup, add ½ cup rice, cook
until rice is fluffy, about 45 minutes
add 1½ cup of the chicken meat.

Dumplings

4 cups bread crumbs
¾ - cup butter - melted
4 - egg - beaten
¼ - t. nutmeg - salt to taste
1 - T. parsley - (if you like it) chopped fine

Combine all ingredients - shape
into ball size of a walnut. Cook as
many you want in chicken broth -
5 - 8 minutes - add to rice soup.
It makes about 50 depending on size
                    left over can be frozen.
(Save some broth to cook dumplings in)

Diet Soup

2 - quarts chopped cabbage
2 - medium Onions, minced
2 -   "   Carrots - grated
1 - lg. green pepper chopped fine
1 - quart V-8 juice
2 -   "   water
1 - t. garlic powder
4 - t. Chicken or beef crystals

Add all ingredients, simmer gently
until Vegetables are tender.

This low-calorie soup could be used as
a between meal snack, or a light meal,
but it doesn't contain enough nourishment
to be used as diet by itself.

Grilled Sandwiches

⅓ cup peanut butter
1-T. sweet pickle relish
2-t. salad dressing
4-strips bacon-crisply cooked & crumbled

In a small bowl mix all ingredients together & spread over 1-side of each bread slice, taking care to cover edges.

Place on foil-broil briefly.
Cut into 2 triangles, serve at once.

Makes 2-4 servings

Strange how one's thoughts turn to food when there is nothing else to think of.

Dutch Oven Sandwiches

1 - 4 lb. rump or brisket of beef
2 - T. oil - plus 1 cup water
1 - sm. can tomato paste
1 - bottle Barbecue Sauce
1 - can beer
1 - Stalk celery - diced
1 - onion chopped
½ - cup brown sugar
½ - t. garlic powder
salt & pepper to taste

Brown beef in oil in heavy pan, add water, cover.
Cook until meat falls off the bone.
remove fat & shred meat.
mix with remaining ingredients.
simmer 1½ hours, covered.

Serves 20 (on buns)

The past cannot be changed.
The future is still in your power.

Pizza Sandwiches

1-lb. ground lean beef
1-Jimmey Dean Pork sausage-veg)
1-medium onion chopped

Brown meat - Onions - drain
add -
1-can sliced mushrooms-drain
4-oz. pkg. shredded cheese
1-14oz. jar Pizza Sauce
mix all together - let cool.

Spoon on split English muffins_
Freeze, get out of Freezer as
you need them_ put them under
broiler 10 minutes, watch so
they do not burn.
            makes 12 Good!

"I love to cook
I love to entertain!
      And
I love the
   compliments
that follow."

32

Delicious Chicken Spread

1½ - cups cooked chopped chicken
1 - cup celery   "
1 - t. onion - minced
¼ - cup chopped pecans
3 - T. mayonnaise
1 - T. lemon juice
¼ - t. curry powder
½ - t. thyme
2 - T. sweet pickle relish
salt & pepper to taste

Combine all ingredients.
Spread between slices of your-
favorite bread.

Can be used as a salad on a lettuce
leaf.

Something good can be said
about everyone - we only have
to say it.

Alligator Stew

1 lb. hamburger
1/4 cup (chopped) onion
1/4 " green bell pepper (chopped)
1/2 " tomato Ketchup
1/2 " water
1 can pork & beans
1/2 cup (or less) brown sugar

Brown hamburger, onion & pepper in skillet. Season to taste, add ketchup, water, pork and beans & brown sugar. Cook until onions & peppers are tender.

Betty Blechschmidt

Very good.!

Salads & Dressings

Mandarin Orange Salad

½ - lg. head lettuce
1 - cup chopped celery
1 - can mandarin Oranges - drained
1 - T. minced parsley
5 - green onions cut up including tops.

Carmalized almonds
¼ - cup sliced almonds
2 - T. white sugar
over low heat stir together till well coated

Dressing
½ - t. salt - dash pepper
2-3 T. vinegar
1 - t. almond extract
¼ - cup salad oil
Shake well in jar v pour over salad just
before serving.

Marian Carew

Vegetable Salad with Toasted Almonds

1-cup green beans
1- " broccoli
1- " asparagus
1- " carrots
1- " sliced celery

Blanch each veggie individually in a pot of water with 1-T. oil until tender.

2-minutes- broccoli, asparagus, celery
6-8 " - green beans, carrots and - cauliflower.

Drain- run cold water over them, add salad dressing and mix well.

Dressing-

½- cup vinegar
2-4-t. sugar (or more)
2-t. sesame oil
1-t. soy sauce
dash of onion powder, garlic, salt & pepper.
¼-cup chopped onions
¼-cup toasted almonds

Sprinkle chopped onions over veggies garnish with toasted almonds.

Cranberry Mousse

1-cup cranberry cocktail
1-3oz. pkg. Raspberry jello
heat cocktail & dissolve jello in it
add -
1-can whole cranberry sauce
1-sm. can crushed pineapple
let cool until it starts to set
add 1-cup cool whip - top with nuts

Sauerkraut Salad

1- large jar kraut
1- cup chopped celery
1- medium onion chopped
1- green pepper   "
1- red   "   "
½- cup cooking oil
½ - " sugar
Drain kraut, mix & refrigerate.

Friends who take time-to-care
are really
angels — unaware.

Creamy Potato Salad

6 - medium potatoes
1 - cup thin sliced celery
½ - onion chopped fine
⅓ - cup sweet pickles chopped
1 - cup mayonnaise
2 - T. sugar
2 - t. celery seed
2 - T. vinegar
2 - t. prepared mustard
1½ - t. salt - pepper to taste
2-4 hard boiled eggs, coarsely chopped

Cook potatoes in salted water until
tender, drain, peel & cube them, add
celery, onions & pickles.
Combine rest of ingredients, add
to potatoes, toss lightly - fold in
chopped eggs.
   Cover & chill thoroughly.
                  Makes 8-10 serving
                     Neil Selzer

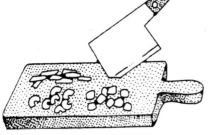

Triple Orange Salad

2 - cups boiling water or fruit syrup
1 - 6oz. Orange jello - sugar free
1 - pt. orange sherbet
2 - cans mandarin Oranges - drained
1 - 13½ oz. can crushed pineapple
1 - cup coconut
1 - cup miniature marshmallows
1 - cup sour cream

Pour boiling liquid over jello, stir until dissolved, add sherbet, stir until melted, stir in mandarin Oranges, chill until firm.

Combine remaining ingredients, fold in Sour Cream - spread over jello, chill well.

41

Cranberry Frozen Salad

8oz. - cream cheese
2 - T - salad dressing
1 - can whole cranberry sauce
1 - 9oz. can crushed pineapple
½ - cup chopped walnuts
1 - cup whipped cream

Mix all ingredients, gradually fold in whipped cream, pour into 8"x 8" dish. Freeze.

Take out of freezer as needed.

Some people, no matter how old they get never loose their beauty.
They merely move it from their face to their hearts.

42

Chicken Fruit Salad

3 - cups cubed cooked chicken
1 - sm. can mandarin Oranges - drained
1 - 8¾ oz. can tidbits pineapple -   "
1 - cup seedless grapes - cut in half
1 - cup fine diced celery
2 - T. orange juice
2 - T. vinegar - little salt
¾ - cup mayonnaise
¼ - cup slivered almonds - toasted

mix all ingredients - serve on lettuce,
garnish with almonds.

Corn Salad

15- ears sweet corn
1- chopped onion.
1- Can Black beans
1-2 cups salsa
¼ - cup western dressing

Cook sweet corn until tender.
Put hot corn in ice water and let cool.
Cut corn from ears and mix with
remaining ingredients, refrigerate,
will keep up to a week.

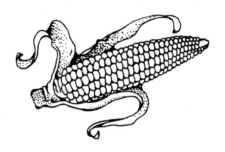

Grape, almond Broccoli Salad

4 - cups broccoli chopped
1 - cup celery   "
1 - cup seedless red grapes
1 - "   "   green   "
⅔ - cup slivered almonds
4 - strips bacon - Cut in bits - fried
½ - cup green onions chopped

Dressing -
1 - T. Vinegar
⅓ - cup sugar
1 -   "   mayo

Prepare all 7 ingredients - place in large bowl. mix ingredients, add dressing, toss just before serving.

"Giving and forgiving"...
   marks of a Christian

Crown Jewel Salad

1- 3 oz. pkg. ea. lime, Orange & strawberry.
or raspberry jello.
3- cups boiling water
1½- cups cold water
mix-
1 pkg. 3 oz. lemon jello
¼- cup sugar
1- cup pineapple juice
½- cup cold water
8 oz. - cool whip

prepare- 3 jellos, using 1 cup boiling
water & ½- cup cold water for each pkg.
Pour into separate 8"x 8" foil pan.
Chill till firm, then cut in ½" cubes.

Heat pineapple juice to boiling, add
sugar & lemon jello, stir, add ½ cup cold
water.
Chill until syrupy.
Fold coolwhip into syrupy lemon.
jello and then fold in jello cubes -
spoon into 9 X 13 pan.

This was served at the 75th. anniversary.
at St. John's Bazaar Luncheon.
10-15-1994

46

Oma's Cucumber Salad

3 - medium cucumbers
1 -   "   Onion sliced
1 - T. salt
⅓ - cup cream or ½ + ½
3 - T Vinegar
Salt + pepper   1-2 · T. mayo

Peel cucumbers - slice thin, add onions
and 1 - T. salt mix let stand 1 hour, drain
mix vinegar, cream + mayo, add cucumbers
a dash pepper.
I add dressing just before serving -

Carrot Salad

3-4 large carrots grated
1-8oz. can Pineapple tidbits-drained
1/3-cup raisins
1/2-cup coconut
1-cup sour cream
1/2-cup nuts-chopped
2-t. sugar

Mix all ingredients together
and chill.

Serves 6-8

5-cup Salad

1-cup mandarin oranges-drained
1-cup pineapple chunks-drained
1-" commercial sour cream
1-" miniature marshmallows
1-" coconut

Combine all ingredients-refrigerate
for 24 hours before serving.
It is rich, but delicious.

Blessings come in many ways
and the nicest come as "Friends".

56

Blueberry Salad

2 - 3oz. Berry Blue jello
1 - #2 can crushed pineapple - undrained
1 - 16oz. blueberry pie filling
1 - cup sour cream
8oz - soft cream cheese
½ - cup sugar
1 - t. vanilla
½ - cup chopped nuts

mix jello in 2 cups boiling water until
dissolved. add pineapple & pie filling.
stir well & pour in 9"x13" pan. Refrigerate.
until set. mix sour cream with cream-
cheese, sugar & vanilla.
spread on top of gelatin.
Sprinkle with nuts.

Fresh Broccoli Salad

2 - bunches fresh broccoli, chopped
1 - small red onion chopped
1 - cup raw, unsalted sunflower seed
6-8. slices bacon, cooked & crumbled
⅓ - cup raisins

mix all ingredients well.

Dressing –
1 - cup mayonnaise
½ - cup sugar (or less)
2 - T. rice or cider vinegar
mix together well.

makes 1½ cups. good.

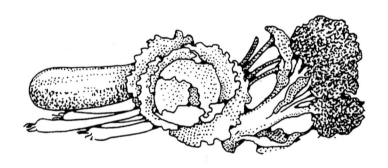

Champion Tuna Salad

1 - 5 oz. can chunk tuna - drained
1 - stalk celery - chopped
¼ - cup mayonnaise
1 - T. lemon juice
1 - t. curry powder
¼ - cup chopped peanuts

Combine tuna & chopped celery in a medium bowl.

In a small bowl, combine remaining - ingredients, except chopped peanuts, add mayo mixture to tuna, mix well, add peanut pieces, mix well.

Serve on a lettuce leaf or a sandwich filling.

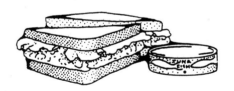

Lord, thank you for your assurance, that you are with us and giving us hope. Amen.

Dandelion Salad

1-qt prepared dandelion greens -
use only young tender plants - discard
leaves that do not look nice - fresh-
they may taste bitter. Try to keep them
in bunch, cut them in ½ inch slices
wash thoroughly - 4-5 times.

3 -T. margarine
1- medium chopped onion
3 -T. flour

saute onions & flour be careful so that
it does not burn, when it starts -
turning color add - ¾ cup water to
which you add 2 -T. vinegar, ½ t. salt
½ t. sugar & dash of pepper, let boil for
2 minutes. Remove & put in salad
bowl, add 2 hard boiled eggs (sliced)
if sauce is too thick - thin with -
buttermilk or half & half, be careful
not to get it too thin.
add dandelion green & toss - if you
like crumbled bacon add it.

It is lots of work - but good eating.
(can substitute endive)

Strawberry Spinach Salad

2- Chicken breast - cooked, boned, chilled -
cut in 2" slivered pieces.
1- apple diced
¼ - cup celery diced
1- cup strawberries - sliced
Combine above ingredients in a bowl

1-cup strawberry yogurt
½ - " slivered almonds
½ - " honey or sweetener
1- T. lemon juice
Mix, this together - pour over above
mixture ↩ toss to cover.
Need -
1- bunch fresh spinach
1- Orange, cut in round slices
1- cup slivered almonds.

   Arrange spinach on platter, then
Orange slices, add chicken mixture.
Sprinkle ½ of almonds on top.

Dorothy Seifert

Smoked Turkey Supreme

12 oz. - Smoked turkey breast -
cut in 1inch strips.
4oz. - Swiss cheese - cut in 1" strips
1 - cup seedless grapes
¾ - cup toasted almonds

Combine, the 4 ingredients.

Dressing -
⅓ - cup mayo
⅓ - cup sour cream
2 - T. milk
  Salt - pepper to taste
mix store in refrigerator

        Serve over lettuce

If you see some one without a smile —
    give him one of yours.

Pea Salad

1- 14 oz. pkg. frozen peas
1- cup cubed mild cheese
1- 6 oz. pkg. salted peanuts
⅓- cup chopped celery
¼ - cup   "   Onions
1ea.- T. red & green peppers
1-hard boiled egg

Dressing-
4 -T. salad dressing
1 -t. lemon juice
1 -t. salad mustard
1. t. celery seed

Combine all ingredients & chill overnite.
I, added some vinegar.

Lord, thank you for protecting us at all
times, wherever we go or whatever we
do. Amen.

Spinach Salad

1-lb. fresh washed spinach
1-can bean sprouts
6-strips bacon, cooked & crumbled
1-can water chestnuts
2-hard boiled eggs sliced
1-medium onion chopped

Dressing-

½ - cup salad oil
¼ - cup sugar
⅓ - cup ketchup
¼ = cup vinegar
2-T. Worcestershire sauce
½ - cup mayonnaise

Blend all dressing ingredients in a
blender for 2 minutes.
Wash & dry spinach leaves, lay in -
refrigerator, tear when cool, add drained
sprouts & water chestnuts, mix together.
add eggs & bacon, dressing last.

The biggest room in the world is
the room for improvement.

Holiday Salad

1 - 3oz. pkg. raspberry jello - sugar free
2 - cups boiling water
1 - can cherry-pie filling
1 - 3oz. lemon jello - sugar free
1 - 3oz. pkg. cream cheese
⅓ - cup mayonnaise
1 - 8½oz. can crushed pineapple - undrained
1 - cup mix. marshmallows
½ - cup whipped cream or cool whip
¼ - cup chopped pecans.

Dissolve raspberry jello in 1 cup boiling water,
stir in pie filling turn into 9"x13" dish, chill
until firm.
Dissolve lemon jello in 1 cup boiling water. Cool.
Beat cheese & mayo until blended,
gradually add lemon jello, stir in pineapple
and marshmallows.
Chill until partly set, fold in whipped -
cream, spoon over cherry layer.
Top with pecans. Chill until firm.

Looks pretty and very good

Poppy Seed Dressing

1 - egg
1/4 - cup sugar
1 - T. Dijon mustard
2/3 - cup red wine vinegar
1/2 - t. salt
3 - T. grated yellow onions
2 - cups oil
3 - T. poppy seeds

Combine egg, sugar, mustard, salt,
vinegar & grated onion in bowl of
food processor.
Process for one minute. With processor
still running, slowly pour in oil.
Then stir in poppy seeds and
refrigerate until ready to use.

If life had no clouds, it would have
no rainbows either.

Raspberry Vinegarette

1. 12oz. frozen raspberrys
2. cups white vinegar
1. cup olive oil
2. cups sugar
dash salt & pepper

Blend smooth in blender.

Serve over lettuce cucumbers or
any veggies or fruit.

It costs nothing to say something
nice about someone!!

Pineapple Dressing

1 - egg
3/4 - cup sugar
1 - T. flour
1 - T. Vinegar
1 - T. butter
3/4 - cup pineapple juice
1/4 - " water - dash of salt

Mix dry ingredients together, cream butter -
add well beaten egg - add dry ingredients -
liquid, beating thoroughly until smooth.
Cook over slow heat until thicken, stirring
to prevent burning.

This makes a delicious dressing for waldorf,
fruit or most any kind of green salad.

Marriage is like a Violin - after the
music stops, the strings are still attached.

Oma's Mayonnaise Dressing

1 - cup vinegar bring to boil
add following ingredients well
<u>beaten</u>
¾ - cup sugar
2 - level tablespoon flour
1 - t. dry mustard
¼ - t. pepper
½ - t. salt
3 - eggs
add to boiling vinegar & beat well
let boil a few seconds, then let cool.
Thin with cream or buttermilk,
when cool.

Teach us, Lord to look, then see, to hear,
then listen; to touch, then feel, so we
may better focus on the many miracles
you offer us each day. Amen.

Layered Salad

1-head lettuce, torn into bite size pieces
1-lb. fried bacon - crumbled
1- medium onion chopped
1- head cauliflower - separated into
flowerettes - (washed)
2-cups mayonnaise
¼-cup sugar
⅓- " grated Parmesan cheese
  Salt & pepper to taste.

Layer lettuce, bacon, onions & cauliflower.
mix mayo, sugar, cheese, salt & pepper -
spread over top layer.
Refrigerate in airtight container overnite

To serve - toss well.

Serves 10-12

Glazed Peach Creme

2 - 3oz. pkg. peach jello - sugar free
2 - cups boiling water
¾ - cup cold water
1 - pint vanilla ice cream
1 - 8¾ oz. can sliced peaches - drained.

Dissolve 1-pkg. jello in 1-cup boiling water,
add ¾ cup cold water - save ½ cup of this jello for
later use. Chill until slightly thickened, then
pour in a serving bowl. Chill.
Dissolve remaining jello in boiling water
add ice cream, stir until smooth - pour
on top of clear set jello in serving bowl. Chill.

Arrange peaches on jello-ice cream mixture.
Top with rest of clear jello - let set.
Serve topped with cool whip - sprinkle w/nuts

Makes 8-10 servings

Life is hard by the yard;
But by the inch, life's a cinch.

Amana Dressing - good on
   Lettuce, Cole Slaw, & Cucumbers -
Combine -
2-3 tablespoons vinegar
½ - cup half & half, in a 4 cup bowl,
let stand 3-4 minutes until thick.
Add.
2 - heaping tablespoons of lite mayo.
⅓ - cup butter milk
1 - teaspoon salt, 2-teaspoons sugar
2 - shakes pepper, 2-shakes mrs Dash.
                    (Original Blend)
Take a handbeater, whip until smooth,
taste & adjust seasoning, if not thick
like heavy cream, add 1 more T. mayo.

For special taste, add 2-T. lite cool whip.
beat again until smooth, makes about
2-cups. Will keep in refriger tor 2-3 weeks.

To lettuce, add 1-sliced hard boiled egg,
some diced onions, or crumbled bacon,
then add dressing, just before serving.

Lord, thank you for filling our hearts with
Your love & peace. Amen.

Oriental Salad

1 pk. Ramen Chicken soup mix
 Combine seasoning pk. with the
following ingredients.
⅓ cup salad oil
2 T. sugar
3 T. vinegar
1 t. salt - Dash of paprika
½ t. pepper or mrs. Dash _original_.

 Brake up noodles, mix with—
ingredients, let stand ½ hour.
 Add.
1 pk. broccoli slaw
2 green onions or medium onion sliced
3 T. toasted sesame seeds
3 T.   "   sliced almonds
½ cup frozen uncooked peas or
 chinese pea pods, & sliced red
peppers for color & taste.

 This is best if it sits overnite
stir or mix a few times,
Holds well for a long time a week.
                    Serves 10-12
     Elsie Oehler

Blessed are they with a cheery
Smile who stop to chat for a little
while.

64A

Sumi Salad

1 pk. Ramen noodles (chicken flavor)
  Combine in large bowl, seasoning pk.
½ cup salad oil
2 T. Sugar
3 T. Rice Vinegar
2-3 T. Soy sauce & broken up noodles
  mix let stand 20-30 minutes

  Then add —
1 Head of Cabbage finely chopped or
1 pk. Cabbage, carrots & red cabbage
½ Onion chopped or sliced
½ cup pecans, almonds or walnuts
Toss. Cover, chill overnite.
mix 2 or 3 times.

  Top with mandarine Orange
segments before serving.

648

Bread & Coffee Cake

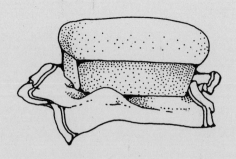

Butter Horn Rolls

1 - cup milk
1/4 - " butter
1 - pk. yeast
3 - eggs
1/3 - cup sugar
1 - T. salt
Flour - to make a soft dough.

Heat milk, add butter to melt - then cool
till lukewarm.
Add 1-T. sugar to yeast, stir until softened.
beat eggs, add sugar & salt, milk & yeast.
Stir in flour to make a soft dough, let rise
until double in bulk.
Roll out & cut pie shaped strips, roll up
beginning with large end

      Bake 400° - 15 minutes

March 10 - 1941 By Miss B. Strawn

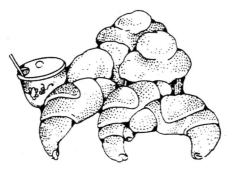

Seasoned bread sticks

1 - 16 oz. unsliced french bread
6 - T. margarine
1 - t. paprika
¼ - t. garlic salt
2-3 T. Parmesan cheese

Cut bread into 1"x1"x4" strips, brush sticks with margarine, cover with rest of ingredients.

Bake 375° 6-8 minutes or until crisp & brown.

Makes 32 sticks

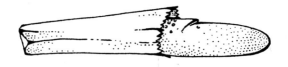

House work is something you do that nobody notices, unless you don't do it.

French Coffee Puffs

2/3 - cup raisins
1/3 - cup soft shortening
1/2 - cup sugar
1 - egg
1/2 - cup sour cream
1½ - cups sifted flour
1½ - t. baking powder
1/2 - t. cinnamon
1/2 - t. salt

Rinse & dry raisins, chop coarsely.
Beat sugar, shortening & egg until well
blended. Blend in sour cream. Sift flour
with baking powder, salt & cinnamon
directly into creamed mixture.
Stir in raisins. Fill muffins tins 2/3 full
          Bake 325° - 20 minutes
while hot dip in melted butter
then in spicy coating, it will take at
least ½ cup butter.
Spicy coating—
½ - cup sugar
mix with
1-t cinnamon

                    Irma Hess

Johnny Cake or Corn Bread

3 - cups yellow corn meal
1 - cup flour
¼ - cup sugar
1 - t. salt
1½ - t. baking soda
3 - t. baking powder
2 - eggs - beaten
2½ - cups butter milk
6 - T. melted margarine
mix -
Dry ingredients.
Combine, eggs, butter milk,
margarine - add to dry ingredients
stir lightly - pour into greased
shallow pan or muffin tin.
          Bake 425° 25 mins.

Pumpkin Nut Loaf

2 - cups flour
2 - t. pumpkin pie spice
2 - t. baking powder
½ - t. " soda - dash salt
2 - eggs
1 - t. vanilla
1½ - cups (solid pack) pumpkin
½ - cup sugar
½ - cup brown sugar
⅓ - " evaporated skim milk
1 - T. oil
¾ - cup chopped nuts

Combine - first four ingredients -
blend eggs, pumpkin, sugar, oil & milk in
a mixing bowl, add flour mixture - mix
just until moistened.
Pour into 9 x 5 inch loaf pan, sprinkle with
nuts.   Bake 350° 1 hour.
     Makes 1-loaf - 16 servings
Variety - add ½ cup coconut -
                    or Chocolate Chips

Lord, thank you for your everlasting
   love and guidance. Amen.

71

No Knead Dinner Rolls

1/4 - cup butter
1 - cake yeast
2/3 - cup lukewarm milk
2/3 - "   "   water
1 - egg.
6 - T. sugar   1 - T. salt
4 - cups flour

melt, butter, mix water, milk, egg
sugar, salt, & yeast, add flour.
use electric mixer to put above
ingredients together. Cover bowl, let rise
until double. Punch down and -
refrigerate until needed.
Shape as desired.

      Bake 375° - 15-20 mins
      depending on size.

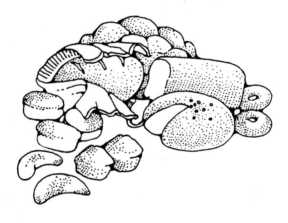

Banana Bread &
Zucchini Bread

2-cups sugar
1-cup margarine
4-eggs
2-cups mashed bananas
1½- " butter milk
2- " Oatmeal
3½- " flour
2- t. baking soda
1- t. vanilla
1- cup chopped nuts

Cream margarine, add sugar, eggs.
vanilla, bananas & Oatmeal - then -
alternatly add flour & buttermilk
then add nuts.
   Bake in 4 loaf pans 350° - 45-50 min

For Zucchini Bread
Sub. - 2 cups shredded Zucchini plus
1-cup coconut instead of bananas.

loaf pans
   should be
      greased.

Angel Biscuits

1 - pkg. dry yeast
¼ - cup warm water
2½ - cups flour
½ - t. baking soda
1 - t. „ powder
1 - t. salt
⅛ - cup sugar
½ - cup shortening
1 - cup buttermilk

Dissolve yeast in warm water, put all dry ingredients in bowl and mix. melt shortening, add to flour mixture. add yeast & buttermilk blending, but not over blending.

Refrigerate until needed. When you want, make some, roll out dough on a lightly floured board & cut with round cutter little biscuits let rise 10-15 minutes. Pop in 400° oven 12-15 minutes.

Oat Bran Muffins

2 - cups oatbran - cooking kind
1 - cup 100% Bran - cereal
1 - " Oatmeal
1 - t. cinnamon
1 - t. baking soda
mix and set aside
micro on high 2 minutes
1 - cup water - 1½ cup raisins - let cool.
then add -
1½ - cup unsweetened applesauce.

In another bowl - beat
2 - egg whites
1 - T. oil
1 - t. vanilla
1 - cup buttermilk

mix all ingredients spoon in
greased muffin pan.

Bake 425° 10 - 12 minutes
Do not over bake.
can add ½ cup nuts or
chocolate chips.

Bran Muffins

1- 15oz. Box Raisin Bran
2- cups sugar
4- egg (beaten)
5- cups flour
1- cup oil
1- quart butter milk
5- t baking soda
2- t. salt

mix bran, sugar, salt & soda, add eggs oil & butter milk.
mix well & add flour. mix in a large container. Store, covered in - refrigerator. use as desired.
Store at least 6 hours before using.

Bake 400° - 15 mins

a Hug is a perfect gift. "One size" fits all" & no body minds if you exhange it.

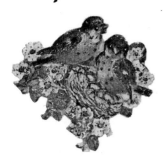

76

Grandmothers Coffee Cake

½ - cup shortening
1½ - cups sugar
2 - cups flour & 2 - t. baking powder
mix together till it is crumbly -
fill a small cup & set aside
add to the above
¾ - cup milk & 2 - eggs
stir and put in greased pan
sprinkle with the Crumbs that are in cup.   Bake 350°   30 - 45 minutes
depending on size of pan.

This is from the Moershel Aunts
              Grandmother

Lord, thank you for guiding us toward
fulfilling our many obligations. Amen.

Nut Bread

2 - cups brown sugar
2 - „ butter milk
1 - egg - beaten
4 - cups flour
1 - t. baking soda - dash salt
2 - t. „ powder
1 - cup chopped nuts
1 - „   „ dates

Sift flour, b. soda, b. powder together.

mix all ingredients, let rise 15 minutes
and bake in slow oven 1 hour.
I grease 2 loaf pans.

          Bake 325° - 1. hour.

What we are is God's gift to us, & what
we (be-come) is our gift to God.

Twice Blessed Cinnamon Rolls

1- pkg. yellow cake mix
5½ - cups flour
mix together in large bowl
Dissolve —
3 pkg. dry yeast & 1-T sugar in ½ cup warm water
add this to flour mixture - plus 3 cups warm
water & 1½ cups margarine.

Knead dough well. it will be sticky. Place
in a oiled pan, also oil top of dough let
raise. I refrigerate dough over nite - but
I first let it raise. on a floured board
roll out dough - (2-3 cups) at a time - brush
with melted butter, sprinkle with sugar
and cinnamon mixture.

mix —
1- cup brown sugar
3- t. cinnamon - ½ cup melted butter
Roll out dough - brush with butter
sprinkle with sugar, cinnamon,
roll dough up & cut in 1" slices.
Place on greased cookie sheet
let rest for 1 hour

Bake 350° 20-25 mins

Ginger Bread

1- cup brown sugar
2- T. molasses
4- T. melted butter
1- egg
1- cup sour cream
2- cups flour
1- t. baking soda
1- cup raisins
1- t. salt, cinnamon, ginger
½- t. nutmeg - cloves

Cream first 3 ingredients, add egg
sift flour, soda, salt, & spices, add flour
mixture & sour cream.

Bake 350° in greased loaf pan
depending on size 1 or 2 45 mins or until
done.

Brown Sugar Icing

1½ - cup brown sugar
⅓ - " water
Cook till it threads, take of stove
beat in 2 T. cream, beat until smooth,
then frost.

my sister Helen Wolf.

80

Oma's Stollen

13 - cups flour
2½ - cups sugar - 2 T. salt
3 - pkg. dry yeast
2 - sticks butter & ½ cup oil.
5 - cups milk
1½ - lbs. chopped dates
1 - box white raisins
1 - " dark "
3 - cups hickory or pecan nuts - chopped

Dissolve yeast in ½ cup warm water plus
2 T. sugar
Measure flour, salt, sugar in large pan.
Add metled butter, oil, warm milk and
dissolved yeast. Mix with wooden spoon,
then knead for 8 minutes or until smooth -
Add dates, raisins & nuts - knead until well
mixed, let raise overnight - cover with
towel.
Put in greased loaf pans, brush with butter,
Sprinkle with sugar, let rest 1 hour
            Bake 350° ½ - 1 hour depending
            on what size pan.

Man cannot live by bread alone, but he
can do all right if he just has plenty of dough.

81

The Best Cinnamon Rolls

1 pk. Vanilla Pudding 3oz.
1 stick margarine - 1 - T. salt
2 pk. dry yeast
½ cup warm water
2 T. sugar
2 eggs beaten
8 cups flour

Mix pudding per. instructions
when thick add margarine, salt,
let cool. Mix yeast in warm water
let stand 5 min.

Add eggs to pudding mixture, also
yeast. Mix well add flour, knead.
Let rise 45 mins.
This will make 2 rolls.
Roll out to 8 x 10 inches
spread with butter or oleo &
brown sugar, cinnamon -
Roll up cut 1" slices. Place on
greased cookie sheet, let rise
15 - 20 mins.

          Bake 350° 20 mins
may take longer depending
on stove.

82

Meats & Casseroles

CHOPPED MEAT

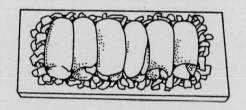

Shredded Beef

1-lb. boneless chuck beef
1-cup water
6-pepper corn
1-Onion - salt to taste
1-crushed clove of garlic
Boil- 1½-hours-until very tender.

In a large skillet heat.
1-T. oil
1-chopped onion
1-crushed garlic
Saute until transparent.
Add 2 small tomatoes -peeled & chopped
1 can mild chopped green chilies,
¼-t. cumin & ¼-t. salt, cook until tender.
When meat is tender cool in broth.
With 2 forks, pull meat apart - save ½ cup broth
then add all ingredients - simmer until
meat is warm, add reserved broth if needed.

Can add some salsa sauce for mexican
flavor - good for sandwiches or mexican food.
Can freeze.
I double the recipe.

Apricot Baked Ham

½ - fully cooked ham with bone 5-7 lbs.
20 - whole cloves
½ - cup apricot preserves
3 - T. dry mustard
⅓ - cup packed light brown sugar

Score the surface of the ham with shallow diamond-shaped cuts. Insert cloves in cuts. Combine - preserves & mustard; spread over ham. Pat brown sugar over apricot-mixture. Place ham on a rack in a roasting pan. Bake 325° - 20 minutes per pound or until ham is heated through & thermometer reads 140°

yield: 10-14 servings

Chicken Almond Bake

3- cups diced cooked chicken
1- can cream of mushroom soup
½ cup evaporated milk
1- " minced celery
1- " " Onions
1- t worcestershire sauce
1- cup blanched slivered almonds
½ -can Chinese noodles for bottom of dish
½ - " " " " top " "

Blend Chicken, soup, milk, add celery, Onions,
worcestershire sauce & almonds.
Sprinkle noodles in bottom of greased
Casserole, spoon chicken mixture on top.
Sprinkle rest noodles on top.

Bake 350° 40-50 minutes

I also add 1 can of mushrooms - drained

Hamburger Stroganoff

1 - lb. ground beef
½ - cup minced onions
1 - clove garlic minced
2 - T. margarine
½ - t. salt - dash pepper
1 - can mushroom pieces - drained
1 - " Cream of celery soup
1 - cup plain yogurt
Some minced parsley
1 - 8oz. pkg. noodles - cooked according
to direction on package.

Saute onions, garlic, add beef brown-
lightly. pour off drippings - season with
salt & pepper, add mushrooms cook 5
minutes, add undiluted soup -
simmer uncovered 10 minutes.
Add yogurt, parsley and cook just
until throughly heated.

Blessed are they who know that my
ears today must strain to catch the
things they say.

Seafood Pasta

3 oz. - shrimp
2 oz. - clams
2 oz. - crab
3 oz. - white fish
1½ - cups clam juice
1 . T. parsley
1 - t . fresh garlic
1 - t . white pepper
1 . T. italian seasoning
3 - cups linguine noodles, cooked
Parmesan cheese

Place all fish items & clam juice in a
medium - one handle pot & bring to a
full boil, add all seasonings & stir well.
Let liquid reduce by half, ladle seafood
on top of warm noodles, sprinkle with
Parmesan cheese, garnish with fresh
chopped parsley. yield 1 - portion

Squirrel or Rabbit

4-6 Squirrel
2-3 Onions
Vinegar
Kitchen Bouquet
Beef gravy seasoning
1-can mushrooms
2- heaping T. flour

Slice onions 1/4" thick, place layer in bottom
of roaster. Place squirrel on top of onions.
Put rest of onions on top of squirrel.
Bake 350° uncovered 1 hour.
Mix 1/2-cup vinegar - 1 cup water - with
2 heaping T. flour - add 2 tsp beef flavor &
1.T. kitchen bouquet, add 1 cup hot water -
add more water if needed to cover the
Squirrel. Then add mushrooms not drained.
Cook for 1 1/2 hours - or 2 hours until tender
salt and pepper to taste.

                    Lial Selzer

Cover after it has been in the oven for 1 hour.

Enchiladas

12 - corn tortillas
1 - cup oil
1 - 20 oz. can enchilada sauce
1½ - lbs. ground chuck, fried with salt, -
Pepper & garlic powder
1 - lb. longhorn cheese, cubed
1 - Lg. onion, finely chopped

Heat tortillas in hot oil until softened.
Heat the enchilada sauce.
Dip hot tortillas in hot enchilada sauce,
remove to a plate, spread with ground chuck
cheese & onions.
Roll & place in layers in heavy casserole.
(Insert toothpick if enchilada does not
stay rolled.)
　　　　Bake 350° 20 min. or until
cheese melts & onions are soft.
Garnish with olives -
　　　　serve while hot.

Sauerbraten

4-lb pot roast of beef
2-cups cider vinegar
2- " water   3/4-1cup wine
12- peppercorns, 4- bay leaves 4- whole cloves
1½-t. salt - ¼-t. pepper
12 - carrots - cut in strips
6 - onions sliced
12- gingersnaps (3/4 cup crushed)
1-T. sugar

Place meat in bowl, combine vinegar
water, peppercorns, bay leaves, cloves, salt
pepper in a saucepan + heat just to boiling.
cool slightly, pour mixture over meat-
cover bowl tightly put in refrigerator -
marinate for 5 days, turning meat once
a day. Remove meat drain thoroughly
strain + reserve marinate. Put roast in
Dutch oven brown on both sides. add
1 cup of marinate, the carrots + onions
cover tightly + simmer 2 hrs., or until
tender. Remove meat to a warm
platter + keep warm. stir gingersnaps
sugar into liquid in Dutch oven. simmer
for 10 minutes.
This makes a delicious gravy.

                              8-10 servings
2- heaping T. flour to thicken the gravy

92

Beef Roast

Preheat oven to 375°
Put roast (2-3 lbs) in roaster - add
whatever you like - onions, or onion
soup mix - plus ½ cup dry wine. cover.
when oven is hot put roast in - leave
oven on for 1-1½ hours depending on
size of roast, do not open oven door
during that time, turn off oven,
leave meat in until oven is cool.

- Very good & juicy -

Ramona Hoppe

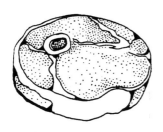

Lord, thank you for granting us a
silent place where we can restore
our peace of mind. Amen.

Oma's Pork Chops

Dip your chops in crumbs then egg and then in crumbs again. you can either fry them in a skillet well done or fry them on both sides and put them in an oven for an hour. you also can put dipped chops raw in a pan, put in an oven they get nice and brown.(uncovered)
Pork must be done never eat it rare.

Oma's baked steak

use round Steak - cut in serving pes. Brown the steak <u>not done</u>, make gravy in the skillet where you browned your steak with a tablespoon flour add water or beef broth, and let bake in the oven for 1 hour in the gravy add salt & pepper. Cover. 325°

Soup Stock

2 - qts. water
2 - T. salt
1 - medium onion or ½ leek
2 - stalks celery - 2 - carrots
add this to either 1 chicken or 2 lb. beef.
Cook until meat is tender. Strain.

Quick Lasagne

1 - lb. ground beef
1 - Jimmy Dean sausage - regular
1 - 15½ oz. jar spaghetti sauce
1 - small box cottage cheese
2 - eggs
6 - oz. shredded mozzarella cheese
8 - lasagne noodles

Cook noodles as directions on box -
drain, rinse in cold water, then dry
on towel. Fry meat, drain, add to sauce.

Layer noodles in bottom 9"x13" dish,
top with meat mixture, ½ of cottage
cheese, ½ of mozzarella cheese, ending
with meat, mozzarella cheese on top, &
sprinkle Parmesan cheese.
"I forgot to mention the 2 beaten eggs
should be add to cottage cheese."
                    Bake 350° ¾-1 hour.

95

Spaghetti Pizza

1 - 7oz. spaghetti - uncooked
½ - cup milk
1 - egg - beaten

Cook spaghetti - drain, toss with milk,
and egg. Spray jelly roll or pizza pan
with oil.

Brown -
½ lb. ground beef.
1 - medium onion - chopped
1 - sliced green pepper
2 - cloves garlic

Add -
1 - 15oz tomato sauce
2 - pkg. italion spaghetti sauce mix
½ - t. mrs Dash - simmer 5 minutes

Layer - Spaghetti, meat sauce,
2 - cups sliced mushrooms
2 - cups shredded cheese.

Bake 350° - 30 minutes

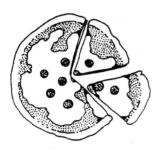

Oma's Chili

1. lb. ground beef
1. onion chopped fine
1 - 2½ can - Kidney Beans
1 - t. chili powder
2. Small cans Tomato sauce
   salt & pepper to taste - also chili powder

Fry the beef, stir to keep fine - stirring
often, add onions, salt + pepper -
add Kidney Beans, chili powder and
tomato sauce - let simmer for
15 minutes

Pizza Meat loaf

1-can tomato soup
¼-cup water
2-3 T. pizza spice
1-cup bread crumbs
½-cup chopped onions
1 - egg - (slightly beaten)
2½ - lbs. ground beef
1-can mushrooms

mix all ingredients except beef and
bread crumbs. add mixture to ground
beef & combine. add bread crumbs to
mixture.
Shape into loaf put into baking pan.
        Bake 350° 1 hour. 15 minutes

Remove from, pour off excess grease and
add mozzarella cheese.
Return to oven & bake until cheese is
melted.

Tuna Cashew Casserole

1 - 3 oz. can Chowmein noodles
1 - can Cream of mushroom soup
½ - cup water
1 - Sm. can chunk style tuna
1 - cup Cashews
½ - " minced onions
2 - Cups cooked rice
salt & pepper to taste

Set aside ½ cup noodles for topping.
Combine rest of ingredients in a
2 quart casserole.
Top with reserved ½ cup noodles.

Bake 350° - 45 minutes
serves - 6

The more of earth we want, the less of
heaven we'll get!

Pot Roast

Tear off enough foil to completely
cover a beef roast.
Sprinkle ½ pkg. Onion soup mix on bottom
of foil, place roast on top & sprinkle
remainder of onion soup mix on roast.
Cover roast tightly with foil and place
on cookie sheet.

   Bake 3-4 hrs – 325° or 6 hrs at 250°

Chicken Cutlets

4 - Boneless Skinless breasts
1 - can golden mushroom soup
1 - " drained - mushroom
1 - cup cooking wine
salt & pepper to taste
In skillet fry c. breasts golden color on both
sides - arrange in casserole.
mix rest of ingredients, pour over chicken
   Bake 350° ¾ - 1 hour or until done.
                  Bill Vaqts

Crab Delight

1-cup cooked peas
4-hard boiled eggs -sliced
2-cups milk
1-8oz. Crab delight — mix all together
Sauce —   salt & pepper to taste
3-T. butter or margarine.
½-cup bread crumbs, mix —
the butter & crumbs — sprinkle over
casserole. Bake 350° 25-30 minutes

Jim Lloyd's Chicken Dish

1½ -cups cooked diced chicken
1 - can cream of celery soup
1 - "   "   " mushroom soup
1 - can mushrooms - drained
1 - 5oz. can Carnation milk
mix all ingredients together.
top with almonds.
           Bake 350° - 30 minutes

Lord, thank you for letting us lean
on you for strength & guidance,
                    Amen.

Chicken Roll

6 - chicken breasts
12 - slices swiss cheese
12 - " thin sliced ham
2½ - cups bread crumbs
⅓ - cup melted margarine
½ - " Parmesan cheese

nite before flatten chicken breasts,
add on each breast 1-slice ham +
1-slice cheese and secure with-
toothpick.
Dip in crumbs + parmesan mixture
cover over nite, store in refrigerater

Bake 350° - 40-50 min

Sauce:
1 - can cream of chicken soup
1 - " mushrooms - drained
½ - cup milk
2 - T. chives
1 - cup sour cream
mix, let come to boil. Serve over
chicken breast, sprinkle with a little
chopped parsley.

Lasagna

1-lb. sweet italian sausage, casing removed and crumbled.
⅔-cup each - chopped onion & fresh chopped parsley.
½-T. fresh minced garlic

Sauce:
3-6 oz. cans Tomato Paste
1-15 oz. can   "   sauce
2-cups water
1½-t. ea. italian seasoning, Oregano & sweet basil leaves

Combine:
1-lb. part-skim Ricotta cheese
1-10 oz. pkg. frozen chopped spinach thawed & squeezed dry.
⅓-cup Parmesan cheese
3-eggs
2-t. garlic salt -¼-t. pepper
12-lasagna noodles, cooked according to package directions.
3-cups shredded mozzarella cheese.

In skillet, brown sausage, onions, garlic & ½ of parsley, drain. Add next 5 ingredients, mix well. simmer, covered 5 mins.
Combine rest of parsley & next 5 ingredients mix well. In 13x9x2 pan, spread 2 cups sauce mixture, layer 4 noodles, ½ cheese mixture, ⅓ sauce & 1 cup mozzarella cheese. Repeat ending w/cheese. Bake 350° - 50-60 mins uncovered.

Hot Chicken Salad Casserole

2 cups cooked cut up chicken
2 " seasoned croutons
1 cup small cut celery
1 " mayo
½ " toasted sliced almonds
¼ " cut (fine) onion
2 T. lemon juice - ½-t. salt
½ cup shredded cheddar cheese
  mix first 8 ingredients.
Put in 2 qt. casserole, 12 x 9. add
cheddar cheese on top
  Bake 30-35 min. uncovered 350°

Cold Cut Roll Ups
Cheese spread — use
Honeyham, smoked ham, or
corned beef slice's,

Spread your favorit cheese on
the surface of a cold cut slice.
Top with pickle, roll up & chill,
cut in 1" pieces to serve.

may need toothpick to hold
  together.

Vegetables & Casseroles

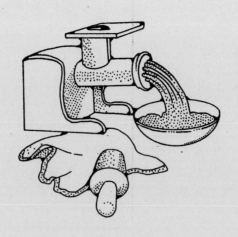

Wild Rice Casserole

1-cup wild rice
1- 10oz. can chicken broth
¾-cup chopped celery
½-cup chopped onions
1-3 oz. can sliced mushrooms-drained
¼-cup butter or margarine - melted
½-t salt
¼-t. pepper

Wash rice several times, place in buttered
1½-quart casserole, add remaining
ingredients, let stand over night.
Stir once during baking.

       Bake uncovered 350° - 2 hours
or until rice is tender.
         6-servings

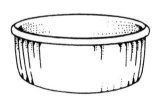

It is difficult to follow -
    God's guidance, if we are on
    rigid paths of our own.

Oma's Amana Spinach

3 - pkg. frozen chopped spinach - if you do not have fresh in your garden

¼ - cup margarine
1 - cup bread crumbs
1 - medium onion chopped
2 - heaping T. flour
½ - t. salt & ¼ - t. pepper
1 - pint or more beef broth

Cook spinach 5-minutes, drain - squeeze out all water, and run through food chopper. Heat margarine over medium heat, add bread crumbs - saute until golden brown - stir in onions & flour, saute a little, add cooked spinach - salt & pepper to taste. Then add beef broth gradually to desired thickness - not too thin Cook until well blended.

Cranberry & Bean Casserole

1-pound ground beef
1-large onion chopped
1- " 20¼oz. can pork & beans
1- 15oz. can cranberries
¼-cup catsup
½- " brown sugar or to taste
  salt & pepper

Brown beef & onions together. Drain.
add beans, cranberries, catsup, -
brown sugar & seasoning.
Pour into 9"x 13" pan.
    Bake 375° - ¾ hour

In the end the love you take, is
equal to the love you make.

Quiche

- 1 - 16 oz. mixed frozen Vegetables
- ½ - cup chopped onions
- 2 - cloves garlic - crushed
- 1 - cup shredded cheese
- 1½ - " milk
- ¾ - " Bisquick mix
- 3 - eggs - can use egg beaters
- Salt & pepper to taste

Heat oven to 400° - spray 10 x 1½" quiche pan. Cook veggies until almost tender drain.
Arrange veggies - I use sausage - mushrooms or whatever you like.
Beat eggs, bisquick, and milk together pour over veggies.
Bake until golden brown & knife inserted in middle comes out clean.
    Bake 350° — 30-35 minutes

Let stand 5 minutes befor cutting.
            good!
            This is a no crust Quiche

Sauerkraut Casserole

1 - lb. ground beef
1 - onion - diced
1 - lg. can sauerkraut
1 - pkg. noodles
1 - can mushroom soup

Brown beef & onions
Cook noodles - drain
Mix all ingredients, add salt & pepper to taste,
Spoon in greased casserole.

Bake 350° 35-40 minutes or until done.

Crusty Bake Potatoes

4 - potatoes - peeled & halved
1 - cup cracker crumbs
1 - t. salt - dash pepper
¼ - cup cooking oil & paprika

Preheat oven 350° - grease baking dish -
mix crumbs, salt & pepper in shallow dish,
dip potatoes in oil - roll in crumbs place
in dish - sprinkle generously with paprika.

Cover bake 350° 1-1½ hours or until done.

Potato Squares

1 - 24 oz. pkg. Hash Brown's - thawed
2 - cups diced ham
6 oz. - Chedder Cheese
6 oz. - Mozzarella ..
3 - beaten eggs or egg beater
½ - t. salt - dash of pepper
1 - cup milk
1 - medium onion chopped

In 9"x13" or larger - greased dish, sprinkle
hash browns, diced ham, cheese, & onions.
Beat eggs & milk, pour over potatoes.

Bake 350° - 1 hour
Cool, cut in squares.

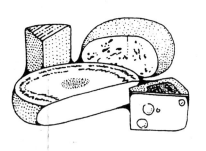

Eggplant Parmesan

1- eggplant peeled & sliced
1- egg-beaten
2- cups crackercrumbs
Dip slices in egg, then crumbs, lay on
a greased cookie sheet. Bake 400° turn once
Saute-
1½- lbs. ground beef
1- medium Onion, drain add
1- can mushrooms, drained & chopped
1- small jar spaghetti sauce - set aside
1- 8oz. pkg. Cheddar Cheese (shredded)
arrange 1 layer eggplant in 9"x 13" casserole
Spoon meat on top, cheddar cheese
sprinkle with Parmesan - repeat with
eggplant, meat, cheese etc. making
3 layers. Bake 350° - ½ hour.

If you make it the day before it will
have to bake 1 hour.

3-Bean Casserole

1. Pound lean ground beef
1-can kidney beans
1-can butter beans
1-can pork & beans
½-cup catsup
¾-cup brown sugar
1-t. dry mustard
2-T. vinegar
1-medium onion-chopped

Brown beef with onions, season with salt and pepper.
Combine the rest ingredients - bake in casserole-top with crumbled bacon.

Bake 350° — 1 hour

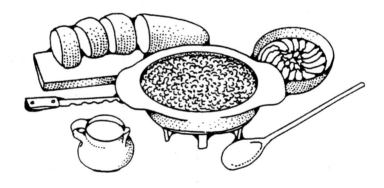

Zucchini Casserole

2- cups shredded Zucchini
3- eggs
½- cup Bisquick
½- cup Velveeta Cheese, diced
½- t. salt
½- t. pepper
¼- cup oil
½- t. garlic powder

Mix all ingredients & bake 350° - 40 mins

Egg Souffle - Sausage

6- eggs slightly beaten
6- slices bread cubed - crust off
1- cup sharp cheese - shredded
2- cups milk
1. t. salt - ½-t. dry mustard
Break up & fry 1-lb. sausage, drain.

Mix all ingredients together, put in
greased 2 qt. casserole.
Refrigerate 12 hours or overnite.
Set out of refrigerater before baking ½ hr.

Bake 350° - 45-60 minutes
check, to be sure if done.
Terry Roemig

Spinach Soufflé

2-pkg. frozen chopped spinach - drained
3-eggs beaten
1-8oz. cottage cheese
¼-lb. American cheese - cut in chunks
2-T. margarine -   "   "   "
3-T. flour

Mix all ingredients.
Spoon into greased casserole.

                    Bake 325° - 1½ hours

You can make day before - then
bake when you have dinner

Stuffed Potatoes

4 - large baking potatoes
½ - cup plain yogurt
2 - T. skim milk
4 - T. snipped chives
½ - t. salt & dash of pepper
½ - t. garlic powder
4 - T. parmesan cheese
dash of Paprika

Scrub potatoes, prick with fork.
Bake 375° 1 hour or until done, slice in
half - scoop out inside - mash potatoes
add yogurt, salt, pepper, milk, chives -
garlic powder and beat until fluffy.

Spoon into potato shell, sprinkle -
with cheese and paprika.
Return to oven - bake until hot &
cheese is melted. 15-20 minutes
          makes 4-6 servings

Lord, thank you for these moments of
prayer, bringing to us peace, hope & a
deepening faith. Amen.

Original Green Bean Casserole

1- Can (10¾ oz) Cream of mushroom Soup
½- cup milk
4- cups cooked green beans
1- t. soy sauce (optional)
Dash of pepper
1⅓- cup French's French Fried Onions.

In 1½- qt. Casserole, mix Soup, milk, soy,
pepper, beans & ⅔ cup Onions.
     Bake 350° 25 minutes, or until hot.

Stir: Sprinkle ⅔ cup onions over bean
mixture. Bake 5 minutes, or until
onions are golden. Serves 6.

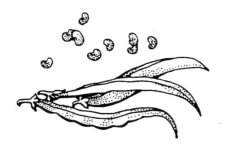

Lord, thank you for the comfort you
bring in times of crisis. Amen.

Unique Corn Bake

1 - 17oz. can creamed corn
1 - 17oz. " whole kernel corn - drained
2 - eggs
½ - cup butter - cut into cubes
1 - cup sour cream
1 - 8½ oz. box - corn muffin mix

mix all ingredients & pour into 9"x 13"
greased pan   Bake 350° - 30-35 minutes

Rebecca Selzer

Is'nt it amazing all the people who come
to Wall Street to clean up and end up being
washed up?

Reuben Casserole

27 oz. jar sauerkrout- drained
1- large tomato sliced
¼- cup Thousand Island dressing
12- oz. sliced corned beef
2- cups shredded American or
Swiss cheese.
¼- cup crushed crackers
¼- t. caraway seed.

Layer in 8" or 9" square baking dish
in order given.
        Bake 425° - 20-25 minutes
    Let stand about 10 minutes

Makes 4 servings
Freeze for up to 2 months.
   Reheat or serve cold.

Harold's Potatoes

6- medium potatoes
1- green onion - chopped
2- cups shredded cheddar cheese
½- cup sour cream
1- t. salt v ¼-t. pepper
¼- cup butter
dash paprika

Cook potatoes with skin, cool, peel~
shred coarsly. In a sauce pan over low
heat, combine cheese and ¼ cup butter,
stir ocassionally until almost melted.

Remove from heat v blend in sourcream
onions, salt v pepper - fold in potatoes
gently and turn into a 2 quart casserole,
dot with butter, sprinkle with paprika

Bake uncovered 350° - 30 mins

Do not over cook potatoes, so they
shred nice.
Annie Kephart.

Lord, give us the strength v guidance so
we may better understand the reasons
for troubled days. Amen.

Red Cabbage

2 - T. margarine
4 - cups shredded red cabbage
2 - apples peeled ⌐ chopped
1 - cup water
4 - T. vinegar
4 - T. sugar
1 - 2. t. salt dash of pepper
2 - T. flour

melt margarine, add cabbage, apples
and water, ⌐ cook until tender.
add blended flour⌐vinegar, sugar
and salt ⌐ cook a few minutes longer.

you can substitute apple sauce for apples.

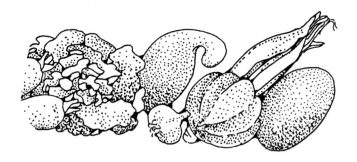

Success is getting up just one more
time than you fall down.

Cakes & Frostings

Rhubarb Cake

Beat-

4 eggs 5 minutes

add-

1-cup oil

2-cups sugar

1-t. Vanilla - beat 5 minutes

Sift together-

2½ cups flour

1½ -t. baking soda & 2-t. cinnamon

add -

6-cups fine cut rhubarb

2½ - cups chopped nuts.

Spread in greased jelly roll pan

Bake 350°-30-35 minutes

When cool, frost with following-

6-T. butter

1½ -cups powder sugar

1 - t. Vanilla

4 -T. hot water.

Lial Selzer

Oma's Chocolate Marble Cake

melt - 3 - sqs - bitter chocolate
add - ¼ - cup boiling water
  4 - T. sugar & ½ - t. baking soda - cool
Sift - 3 - cups flour
  2 - t. baking powder - 3 time
Beat in mixer - until creamy -
  ½ - cup butter & ½ - cup oil
  2 - cups sugar
  4 - eggs - not separated
  1 - t. Vanilla
  1 - can carnation milk - large size

add flour alternatly with milk, then take ½ of batter add to Chocolate mixture mix well. Pour white batter by spoonful in greased bundt pan, alternately with chocolate mixture - after all batter is in take knife, put in batter, go around twice

   Bake 350° - 50 minutes

When baked, take a cake plate put on top & turn over, let sweat for 5 minutes

Frosting for this cake is on next page.

Frosting For Oma's Marble Cake

Melt:
2 - squares bitter chocolate
¼ - cup butter

Add:
1 - t. vanilla
3-4 cups powder sugar
enough cream to make it spread nice,
stir until nice and smooth.

I like to freeze the cake, then frost
while still frozen.

Good Luck!

Polynesian Cake

Beat in mixer –

1 – cup oil

1¼ – cups sugar

3 – eggs

2 – t. Vanilla

2 – sm. jars strained carrots

add –

2 – cups flour

2 – t. Cinnamon

2 – t. baking powder

sifted together 2 · times

add –

1 – sm. can crushed pineapple – drained

½ – lb. coconut

1 – cup chopped nuts

Bake in greased Bundt pan 350° – 50 · 55 min

Cream Cheese Frosting –

3 oz. Soft cream cheese

2 – T. butter

1 – t. Vanilla

2 – 3 cups powder sugar

Thin with little cream to make it spread

nice.

Can use cooked mashed carrots or

grated carrots – 1 cup.

This is a special cake.

Coconut Cake

1. box white cake mix
mix cake according to direction
Add:
1 - cup coconut
1 - t. coconut flavoring
Bake as directions on box - while hot, poke
large holes in cake with a wooden spoon
handle.
Mix,
1/3 - cup water ⎱
1/4 - " sugar ⎰ boil 2 minutes
add - 2/3 - cup milk, then pour over hot cake.

When cod frost with cool whip to which
you add 1/2 - cup coconut + coconut -
flavoring.

Esther Jann
This is delicious
served with fresh
Strawberries.

Poppy Seed Cake

Soak - ⅓ cup poppy seed in 1 cup milk -
overnight.

Cream -

¾ - cup butter

1½ - cups sugar

Sift together -

2 - cups flour

2 - t. baking powder

4 - egg whites - stiffly beaten

Add ingredients in order given, folding
egg whites last.

Bake in layers 350° - 30 minutes

Put together with following filling -

4 - egg yolks

1 - cup sugar

2 - T. cornstarch

1 - cup water

½ - cup nut meats

Mix egg yolks, sugar, and cornstarch.
Add water & cook until thick. When cool,
add nut meats & spread between layers.
Frost with white frosting.

Oma Selzer

130

Self-frosting Zucchini Cake

½-cup margarine
1¾-cups sugar
½-cup oil
2-eggs - 2-cups shredded zucchini
1-t. vanilla
½-cup buttermilk
2½-cups flour
1-t. baking soda
½-t. " powder
4-T. cocoa
½-t. cinnamon

mix first 5 ingredients well.
Sift flour, soda, b.powder, cinnamon &
cocoa together - add sifted flour -
alternately with buttermilk until well
blended.
Sprinkle topping on batter before
baking.
            Bake in greased jellyroll pan
                325° - 30-40 mins
Topping-
½-cup Chocolate Chips
½-cup chopped nuts
¼-cup brown sugar

Oma's Strawberry Short Cake

6 - egg whites stiffly beaten
1 - cup sugar
6 - egg yolks beaten until lemon colored
1 - cup sifted flour
1 - t. Vanilla

To the beaten egg whites, slowly add sugar, beating all time. add beaten egg yolks alternately with flour - beating after each addition. Pour into tube pan that has been well greased a sprinkle with sugar.

Bake in slow oven 275° - 1 hour.

Remove from pan immediately a cool on rack. slice in half.

Filling -
1 - egg white
1 - cup sugar
1 - cup strawberries

Beat until very stiff. on first layer, arrange strawberries that have been sugared, then spread, filling then cake, berries, filling - frost the whole cake with filling - very good! Refridgerate.

132

Lady Golden Glow Cake

½-cup butter
1½-cups sugar
2-eggs - separated
2⅔-cups - flour
4-t. baking powder
1-cup milk
grated rind of ½ orange
1½-squares bitter chocolate - melted

Sift flour, baking powder - set aside.
Cream butter, sugar, 2 egg yolks, grated
orange rind - add sifted flour + milk - fold
in stiff beaten egg white. To ½ of batter add
melted chocolate mix well, spoon in greased
2 round cake pans, alternating white and
chocolate.   Bake 350°   25-30 minutes
Do not over bake. Filling.

3-T. melted butter - 3-sqs. bitter chocolate
3-cups powder sugar
2-T. orange juice - grated rind of ½ orange
pulp of 1-orange - 1-stiff beaten egg white
Beat butter, sugar, orange + rind until smooth
fold in stiff beaten egg white - spread this
on top layer. using a sharp knife shave ½ of
1 chocolate square - sprinkle on top layer.
add rest of melted chocolate to filling,
spread this thickly between layers; on side of
cake. Oma Selzer got this from Katie moershel

Helen's Nut Cake

1½ - cups sugar
½ - cup margarine and ¼ - cup oil
3 - eggs
3 - cups flour
3 - t. baking powder
1 - t. vanilla
1 - large can Carnation milk (lite)
3 - cups chopped walnuts meats (fine)

Cream first 4 items, plus vanilla -
Sift flour and baking powder, add flour
alternately with milk - add nuts.
Pour into 2 greased cake pans
        Bake 350° 25 - 30 minutes

Can also bake in 9" x 13" or in a bundt pan
50 minutes - test to see if done.

Italian Cream Cake

Cream—
½-cup shortening
½- " butter
2-cups sugar
add-
5-egg yolks, one at a time
2-t. Vanilla
Sift together-
2-cups flour
1-t. soda
add alternately with 1-cup buttermilk

Fold in-
5 egg whites stiffly beaten
2-cups Angel Flake coconut
1- " chopped pecans.

Pour into 3 greased pans.
Bake 350°-25 minutes

Frost with Cream Cheese
frosting.

Chocolate Sheet Cake

2 - cups sugar
2. " flour
⅓ - cup cocoa
1 - t. baking soda
1 - cup margarine
1 - " water
½ - " butter milk
2 - eggs - 1- t. vanilla

Combine first 4 ingredients in mixing bowl, mix well.
Heat water & margarine until boiling, pour over dry ingredients. mix beat in eggs, vanilla butter milk - pour in greased 15"x10" jelly roll pan

Bake 400° - 20 minutes
18 servings

Frosting
4 - T. cocoa   — 6 - T. milk - 1-stick margarine
   1- lb. powdered sugar - 1-cup nuts
Bring cocoa, milk, and margarine to a boil & pour over powdered sugar. mix well and add nuts; spread on hot cake.

Lial's Apple Cake

Beat:

4 - eggs - 4 minutes

add - 1 cup oil
- 1 - " brown sugar
- 1 - " white "
- 1 - t. vanilla

beat 4 more minutes

Sift:
- 2½ - cups flour
- 1½ - t. baking soda
- 2 - t. cinnamon

add - to egg mixture
- " - 5 cups peeled diced apples
- " - 2 " chopped nuts

Spread in greased jelly roll pan.

Bake 350° - 30 minutes

When you take out of oven while still hot - you mix ½ cup sugar & 1 t. cinnamon & sprinkle over cake.

The best and most beautiful things in the world, cannot be seen or touched, but are felt in the heart.

Marian's Sugar Plum Cake

2-cups flour	1½-Cup sugar
1½-T. cinnamon	3 - eggs
¼-t. cloves	1-cup buttermilk
1-t. nutmeg	1½- " cooked prunes-cut
1-t. baking soda	in pieces & smashed.
1-cup oil	1-T. vanilla - 1cup chopped nuts.

mix & sift together, flour, spices, soda & salt
Beat oil & sugar together until creamy, add eggs
one at a time. add dry ingredients along with
buttermilk & beat well. add prunes, vanilla &
nuts, Pour in greased tube pan, like angel
food pan where the bottom pulls out from
sides. a bundt pan wont work.

Bake 350° - 60 minutes

Glaze—

1-cup sugar, granular	1-t. soda
1-stick butter	½-t. vanilla
½-cup buttermilk	1-T. white Karo Syrup

Put all ingredients in sauce pan & let come to
a boil, cook 10 minutes, watch closely as this
really bubbles up. Pour over cake while hot.
allow to soak into cake in pan, cool before
removing. Can be eaten plain or frost,
with Caramel Pecans Frosting.

Also good with Cream Cheese Frosting

Frosting for Sugar Plum Cake
Caramel Pecan Frosting

2-cups sugar
1- Cup buttermilk
1- t. soda + ½-t. salt
1- cup pecans chopped fine
2-T. butter

using large pan, as this really bubbles
up, combine sugar, buttermilk, soda+salt.
cook 5 minutes stirring constantly.
add pecans + butter. cook until soft
ball stage 8-10 minutes - don't over cook.
set aside to cool, beat. if frosting gets
hard while frosting, place pan in -
hot water for easy spreading.
Can make ½ recipe if you want to drizzle
over top of cake + run down sides.
Or, left over frosting can be used for
pralines Drop by t. on waxpaper

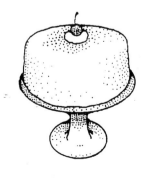

Queen Elizabeth Cake

1 - cup boiling water
1 - cup chopped dates
1 - t. baking soda
Pour boiling water over dates & soda
let stand while mixing cake.
1 - cup sugar
¼ - " butter
1 - egg beaten
1 - t. vanilla
Sift together
1½ - cups flour
1 - t. baking powder
½ - cup chopped nuts

Cream butter, sugar, eggs & vanilla -
add date mixture - then stir in -
flour & nuts.
Bake in 9"x13" greased pan.
350° - 35 minutes

Frosting -
5. T. brown sugar
5. T. cream
2 - T. butter - boil 3 minutes, pour over
cake, sprinkle with coconut & nuts.

Very Good!

Angel Cake

1- cup granulated sugar
1½ -cups powdered sugar
1½ - " egg whites
1- cup cake flour
1½ - t. cream of tartar
¼ - t. salt
1 - t. vanilla
¼ - t. almond flavor

Sift-powder sugar, flour, cream of tartar, salt & sugar 5 times.

Bake 275° - 30 minutes
    " 300° - 30 "

P.S.
"pour batter in ungreased -
angel food cake pan."

Sprinkle with -
        powder sugar

141

Cranberry Pudding Cake

1½ - cups whole cranberry sauce
½ - cup crushed pineapple
1 - T. lemon juice
2 - T. cornstarch
1 - T. sugar

Batter

1½ - cups sifted flour
½ - cup sugar
2 - t. baking powder & ¼ t. salt
3 - eggs, separated
⅔ - cup milk
3 - T. melted butter
3 - T. sugar - slivered almonds if desired

Blend first 3 items together - mix cornstarch & sugar, add to cranberry mixture, blend well. Pour into greased 8 x 8 baking dish.

For batter - sift flour, sugar, b. powder salt. Beat egg yolks, stir in milk & butter, add to flour mixture, blend until flour is well moistened, spoon over cranberry mixture in baking dish.

Bake 350° 35-40 mins.

Beat egg whites add 3. T. sugar - return to oven & bake 12-15 mins longer.

1+2

Dump Cake

1 can Cherry pie filling
1 " crushed pineapple-not drained
     Mix-
pour-in- 9"x 13" cake pan
     Sprinkle-
1 box yellow cake mix over top
of fruit mixture, pat on evenly.
     Add-
1 stick of margarine cut up in
little pieces.
     Sprinkle-
shredded coconut and
chopped nuts over top.
     bake 350° - 40-50 minutes

Serve with Cool whip
     or ice cream.

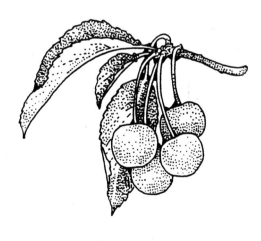

Graham Cracker Cake

½ - cup butter
1½ - cups sugar
3 - eggs - beaten
1 - cup milk
2 - t. baking powder
1 - cup chopped nuts
1 - 1 - pound box graham crackers

mix butter & sugar in a large bowl -
until smooth & creamy.
Add eggs, milk, baking powder &
nuts. mix well.
Crush graham crackers into crumbs.
add to mix in bowl, mix well.
Pour into 2 greased cake pans.

         Bake 375° - 40 minutes
When cool, frost with your favorite -
frosting.

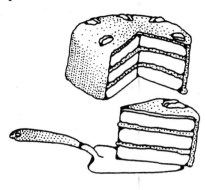

Feather Cake

1 - cup shortening
2 - cups sugar, beat until creamy -
add 3 egg yolks, beat some more.
Sift together -
3 - cups flour
3 - t. baking powder
1 - cup milk
1 - t. Vanilla
3 - egg whites beaten stiff

add flour, milk alternately. add Vanilla
fold in beaten egg whites -
Pour into greased Bundt pan.

Bake 375° - 30 minutes
then 350° until done.

Frost with your favorite frosting.

Aunt Frieda's
Pineapple Upside - Down Cake

1- 8oz. can pineapple rings
2- T. unsalted butter
½- cup dark brown sugar packed
9- maraschino cherries, cut in half
⅓- cup vegetable shortening
¾- cup sugar
1- egg - ¼- t. salt.
1¾- cups flour
2½- t. baking powder
1½- t. vanilla
icecream or whipped cream

Preheat oven 350°. Drain pineapple reserving the liquid. melt butter in a deep 9" oven-proof skillet. Stir in the brown sugar + 1-T. pineapple juice. Arrange pineapple rings in the pan, filling all centers with cherry halves. Set aside. Beat shortening, sugar, + eggs together, until well blended 3-4-minutes. Combine flour, salt baking powder. measure pineapple juice and enough water to make ⅔ cup. add dry mixture + juice to shortening mixture alternately + beat. Pour over Rrings place in oven - Bake 350° 43 minutes or until done in the middle. Cool 5 mins. before running a knife around edge + inverting cake onto a plate. Serve with ice cream or whipped cream.   makes 6-8 servings

Crumble Cake

2 - cups brown sugar
¼ - t. salt
2 - cups flour
1 - t. cinnamon
1 - scant cup butter or margarine
mix till crumbly

Take ¾ cup crumbs out for the top,
put aside, to the rest add -
1 - egg
1 - t. baking soda dissolved in -
1 - cup sour milk or buttermilk. mix
pour in 2 greased pans - sprinkle
crumbs on top & bake

Bake 350° - 25 minutes

I bake it in 2 - 8" round pans.

Lord, thank you for another new
          sunrise. Amen.

Oma Selzer's
Burnt Sugar Cake

First-
1-cup sugar- pour in black skillet, stir
while it is melting-as it starts turning golden
pour in ½-cup water, stir until smooth.
Set aside.

1-cup sugar
½- " butter
2-eggs-separated
2-t. vanilla
1-cup milk
2½-cups flour ——— sift the
2-t. baking powder) 2 together
mix all ingredients together
Beat 2-egg whites

Pour burnt sugar into cake batter.
stir until smooth- then fold in stiff
beaten egg whites- bake in greased
pan 9"x 13" or 2 round pans.
                Bake 350° 35-40 minutes

Frosting-
1½-cups sugar — 1-cup milk
1-T. butter   - 1-t. vanilla
Cook in skillet where you burned the
sugar-this gives it color & flavoring.
Cook frosting until it begins to thicken
don't cook it too long.

White Chocolate Cake

⅓-lb. white Chocolate (melted)
1-cup butter or margarine
1- " sugar
4- eggs
1- t. vanilla
2½-cups flour
1½-t. baking powder
1-cup buttermilk
1- " chopped pecans
1- " flaked coconut

Cream butter, sugar & chocolate. Add eggs one
at a time, beating well, add vanilla & dry
ingredients alternately with buttermilk.
Stir in nuts & coconut.

Bake in 13"x9"x3" pan 350° 35-40 mins. or
in 2-9" layers 30 mins, or a tube pan 75 mins.
Grease & flour all pans.
Icing:
2-Cups sugar 1-cup margarine. 1-t vanilla
1-Can condensed milk.
Combine all ingredients, mix well & let
stand 1 hour (stir occasionally). Then cook
until it reaches soft ball stage, when tested
in cold water. Remove from heat & beat until
creamy & right consistency for spreading on
Cake.

Upside down Chocolate Cake

Mix together in large mixing bowl.

1- cup flour
1- t. baking powder
3/4- Cup Sugar
1/2 -t. salt
Add and mix in
1/2 - cup milk
2 -T. margarine - melted
1- t. Vanilla
1/2- cup chopped pecans
Pour in 13" x 9 x 2" greased pan.
Mix:
1/2- cup brown sugar
1/2- "   white sugar
1/4- "   cocoa
1 1/4- cups boiling water

Pour over batter.
Bake in preheated oven 350° - 40 minutes

Turn cake pan up side down on plate
while hot, right after it is out of oven.
The boiled ingredients makes the frosting.

Pies and Desserts

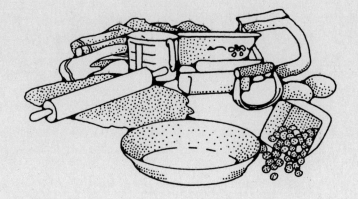

Strawberry Pie

Crust:
½ - cup butter
2 - T. sugar
1 - cup flour
mix press in 9" pie tin - Bake 15-20 minutes

Filling:
1 - cup sugar
3 - T. cornstarch
1 - cup boiling water
1 - 3oz. strawberry jello
mix & stir in boiling water, boil for 3 mins.

Pour over strawberries that have been placed in crust. 2 - pints fresh washed-berries.

Serve with cool whip.

Save your breath giving advice, unless you're a doctor or lawyer and charge for it.

Coconut Pie - makes its own Crust

4 - eggs
1¾ - cup sugar
½ - cup flour
¼ - cup melted butter
2 - cups milk
1½ - cups coconut
1 - t. vanilla

Combine in order given. Pour into greased
10" pie pan. Bake 350° - 45 minutes until
golden brown. Cool.

Apple - Blue Berry Pie

3 - cups sliced peeled apples
2 - cups fresh blueberries
1 - cup brown sugar
½ - cup white sugar
⅓ - cup flour
1 - t. cinnamon
2 - T butter

Combine all ingredients put in deep
pie crust - Bake 350° 1 hour. You can use
pastry strip lattice on top of pie - or
make it a 2 crust pie.

Sour Cream Raisin Pie

2 - eggs well beaten
1 - cup sugar
1 - T. flour
1 - cup sour cream
1 - t. vinegar
1 - box raisins
½ - cup nuts - if you like them

mix sugar, flour, add sour cream & eggs - stir well until moistened. add raisins - pour in a unbaked pie crust.

Bake 425° - 10 minutes - then 325° until set - about ¾ hour.

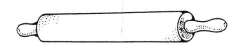

Lord, thank you for filling our lives with faith, hope and love.

Lemon Cake Pie

1. Pie crust - unbaked

Filling -
1. lemon - juice - grated rind (1/4 cup)
1 1/4 - cup milk
1 - cup sugar
2 - T. flour (heaping)
3 - eggs separated
1 - T. melted butter

Beat all ingredients together (except the 3 egg whites that have been beaten stiff, fold in beaten egg whites.
Pour into pie crust, bake in slow oven.

Bake 325° 1 hour or until done

From Elizabeth Geiger Schmieder

This recipe is over 60 years old.
It is good!!

Famous Pumpkin Pie

2 - eggs - slightly beaten
1 - 16 oz. can Pumpkin (Libby's)
¾ - cup sugar
2 - t. pumpkin pie spice
1 - 13 oz. can evaporated milk
1 - 9° deep dish unbaked pie shell

Preheat oven 425°
Mix ingredients in order given
pour into pie shell.

Bake 425° 15 minutes then reduce
heat to 350° bake another 45 mins.
or until knife inserted in center
comes out clean. Cool.
Garnish with whipped topping.

Grated Apple-Pecan Pie

1. cup sugar
1. T. flour 1-t. cinnamon - dash of salt
5. apples - coarsely grated (peeled apples - (4-cups)
1. beaten egg
¼.cup butter or margarine melted
½-1cup chopped pecans
1. 9" Pastry unbaked shell

Preheat oven to 400° - Combine sugar, flour,
cinnamon & salt in large bowl; add apples &
toss gently. Stir in egg & butter. Spoon mixture
into pastry shell.
For firmer crust, brush first with egg white.
Sprinkle with pecans. Bake for 10 minutes - reduce
heat to 350° & bake for 50 minutes.
                    make 8 serving.
When cool serve with cool whip or cream.

Lord, thank you for filling our hearts with
your love and peace. Amen.

158

German Fruit Pie

1-cup sugar
3-T. butter melted
2-T. Vinegar
1-T. water
½ - cup white raisins
½ - cup walnuts or pecans
3- well beaten eggs
1- cup coconut
¼ -t. cinnamon

mix all ingredients together - add eggs
last, pour into unbaked pie crust.

Bake 375° 30-35 minutes.

All-Star Apple Pie

1 can 21 oz. apple pie filling
1 T. spoon lemon juice
¼ t. cinnamon
1 9" pastry shell - baked

¼ cup flour
¼ " packed brown sugar
¼ " chopped pecans or walnuts
¼ " quick oatmeal
4 T. flaked coconut
3 T. butter or margarine - melted.

In a bowl combine pie filling.
lemon juice, cinnamon, spoon into
baked pastry shell. I another bowl
combine flour, sugar, butter until
resembles coarse crumbs, stir
in nuts, oats & coconut. Sprinkle
over pie filling.

Bake 400° 12-15 mins
or until topping is golden brown.
Cover edge of pastry with foil to
prevent getting too dark.

Cool on rack - yields 10-12 pes.
I serve cool whip on top.

Apple Kuchen

1. pie crust
4 - cups apples - washed, peeled & sliced

Filling -
3/4 - cup sugar
2-3 T. flour
1 - egg - beaten
1 - cup carnation milk - lite (Lg can.)
arrange fruit in pie crust.
mix sugar, flour, egg & milk pour over
fruit.   Bake 425° - 15 minutes
then reduce oven 350° - bake until
fruit is cooked & custard is well set.
Before serving can top with cool whip.
good with peach, apricot, raspberries
also good made with rhubarb - use -
1 cup of sugar, for it.

Caramel Crust Dessert

1½ - Cups uncooked rolled Oats
⅓ - Cup brown sugar
2 - T. flour
½ - Cup butter

Mix together oats, sugar, ∟ flour.
Pour melted butter over dry
ingredients, mix well. Pour in a pie
pan or 9"x 13" dish. Bake 350-10·15 min
or until sugar is dissolved ∟ a little
toasted. save ⅓ for topping.
Press remainder in pan, put any kind
of pie filling in (we like blueberry)
top with rest of topping.
serve with whipped cream or
Codwhip -
                good!

Pumpkin Pie Dessert

4 - eggs - slightly beaten
1 - 16 oz. can pumpkin
1½ - cups sugar
2 - t. pumpkin pie spice
1 - t. salt
1 - 12 oz. can evaporated milk
1 - pkg. yellow cake mix
1 - cup margarine - melted
1 - cup chopped pecans

Mix first 6 ingredients, pour into ungreased 9"x13"x2" pan.
Sprinkle dry cake mix over filling, pour melted margarine over cake mix, sprinkle with nuts.

Bake 350° - 1-1½ hours or until knife inserted in center comes out clean.

Serve warm or chilled, plain or with ice cream or whipped topping.

Dorothy Seifert

163

Bread Pudding

2 - eggs, well beaten
½ - cup sugar
2 - cups milk
4 - ½" day-old bread or cake cubes (4 cups)
¼ - cup raisins, if desired

Beat into beaten eggs, sugar, milk.
Butter a 1½-quart casserole, put bread
cubes into casserole, pour egg mixture
over bread. Let stand until bread is
thoroghly soaked. mix in raisins.

Bake 350° 25-30 minutes

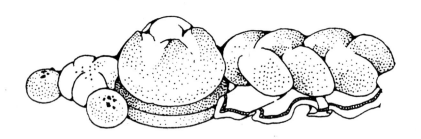

Strawberry or Raspberry Dessert

Topping:
1- Cup flour
½ - cup nuts - chopped
¼ - cup brown sugar
½ - cup melted butter
mix & bake, stir until slightly gold.
and not pressed in the pan, you will
save ½ of mixture for top. Bake 350° - 20 min

Filling:
1- 10 oz. pkg. frozen strawberries or -
Raspberries.
2 - egg whites
⅔ - cup sugar
2 - T. lemon juice
1 - 10 oz. Cool whip

Beat together for 10 minutes - Then fold
in cool whip. line 9"x13" pan with ½ of
topping. Then add filling - top with
the rest of topping.
Freeze for 6 hours or over night.

Very good!

Snow Balls

1 - cup sugar
½ - cup butter
2 - egg yolks - beaten well
1 - cup crushed pineapple
2 - egg whites stiff & folded into
above ingredients.
1 - cup nutmeats. mix all together.
1 - Box. vanilla wafers.

Put filling between 3 vanilla wafers
and let stand awhile.

1 - pint whipping cream or Cool whip.
3 - oz. jar of maraschino cherries.
4 - oz. coconut.

Whip cream & cover vanilla wafers.
sprinkle with coconut and top -
with cherry.

A beautiful dessert for the holidays.
            and
        Scrumptious!

Rice Pudding-Lemon Sauce

1-cup rice ⎫ Cook until tender
¾-quart milk ⎭
½-cup sugar
¼-lb butter
6-eggs - Separated
Cream butter, egg yolks & Sugar, add
to cooled rice. Fold in stiffly beaten
egg whites_pour into greased baking
dish & bake 300° 50-60 minutes.

Lemon Sauce

1½-cup sugar   4-T. cornstarch 4-lemons
3-cups boiling water. 2-t. butter. 3 eggs -
mix sugar, cornstarch & lemon juice,
add boiling water & cook until thick.
(you can cook this in Radarange)
add butter & beaten yolk + remove -
from heat. when cold fold in stiffly
beaten whites.

Homestead Hotel Fritters

½ - cup flour
⅜ - ‚‚ milk
2 - eggs - separated
½ - t. sugar
⅛ - t. salt

Sift together flour & salt, add
milk & egg yolks, beat egg whites
well, until stiff, add sugar slowly &
beat until almost dry, fold into
first mixtur & fry in deep hot
fat until golden brown.

Sprinkle with powder sugar.
Serve immediately.

Lord, thank you for helping us
meet the many challenges that
come our way. Amen.

Yeast Dumplings with Cinnamon Sauce

1-cup milk	2-eggs beaten
½-" margarine	1-pkg. yeast
1-T. sugar	¼-cup warm water
1-t. salt	4-cups sifted flour

Heat milk, margarine, sugar, salt and
beaten eggs. add yeast that has been
dissolved in warm water, add flour & knead
let rise over night in a warm place.
Form dough into dumplings 2" across, let
rise till double in bulk.
Put 1-T. margarine in a heavy skillet-
with tight fitting cover & ¾ cup boiling-
water & 1-t salt. Place dumplings in-
skillet, side by side, cover & simmer
15 minutes without removing lid.
Place in serving dish top bread crumbs
which have been browned in butter.

Cinnamon Sauce

¼-cup sugar	½-cup cold milk
4-T. flour	3½-" scalded milk

1-t. (or more if you like) cinnamon
mix sugar, flour, & cinnamon, moisten
with cold milk, add scalded milk,
cook in top of double boiler until
thick. Serve hot with dumplings.

Pumpkin Dessert

crust:
1-cup flour
½-cup oatmeal
½-cup brown sugar
½-cup butter

filling:
2-cups pumpkin
1-large can evaporated milk
2-eggs
1-t. pumpkin spice

Topping:
½-cup chopped pecans
½-cup brown Sugar

For crust:
mix ingredients & press into 8x8"pan.
Bake 350° - 15 minutes.

For filling:
mix ingredients well & pour over baked
crust.   Bake 350° - 20 minutes.

For topping:
mix ingredients & sprinkle over filling.
Bake 350° - 20 minutes, or
until firm.

when cool cut in squares & serve with
whipped cream or cool whip.

English Trifle

1 - sponge or pound or
1 - yellow cake mix. bake as direction
in 2 layers or Bundt pan
Slice to make 4 layers
Dissolve - 3oz. box lime jello
2 - pkg. frozen red raspberries, drain,
juice, thicken with cornstarch, then
add raspberries.

Custard -
2T. melted butter, add 2 - cups milk
blend 1/4 cup cornstarch & 3/4 - cup sugar
add to milk, cook stirring constantly
until it thickens - remove, add 2 -
beaten egg yolks, cook 2 minutes
longer, add 1 - t. vanilla.

To put together - in large glass bowl.
1 - layer cake
2 - 1/2 of jello
3 - 1/3 of custard
4 - 1 - layer cake
5 - 1/2 - of red berries
6 - 1/3 of custard
7 - layer cake
8 - rest of jello, custard & berries
top cake & whipped cream.
Helen Kraus.

Pecan Pie

1-unbaked pie shell

1½ - cup sugar
¾ - t. salt
1 - cup dark corn syrup
¼ - cup butter
2¼ - t. vanilla
3-cups chopped pecans or hickory nuts
5-eggs, whipped until foamy

mix together sugar, syrup & salt, dissolve
over low heat, add remaining ingredients
in order given, one at a time, stir after
each addition. Pour filling into pie shell.

Bake 325°   1 hour.

Cookies & Bars

Cadillac Brownies

½ - cup butter melted
1 - " sugar
4 - eggs
1 - 16 oz. can Hershey Chocolate syrup
1 - cup flour
½ - T. baking powder
1 - t. vanilla
½ - cup chopped nuts

Blend all ingredients well ~ pour into a buttered 10"x15" jelly roll pan.
                    Bake 350° - 15-20 minutes

            Frosting:
                        Butter Chip icing.
melt -
6 - T. butter
add - 6 - T. milk - bring to boil, stir in
1 - cup Sugar
1 - " chocolate chips.
Beat until creamy - spread over
Cadillacs, when cool, cut in squares.

                    They freeze well.

Chocolate Crackles
moist, fudgy-type cookies

4 - 4 oz. squares unsweetened chocolate
½ - cup salad oil
2 - cups sugar
4 - eggs, unbeaten
2 - t. vanilla
2 - cups flour
2 - t. baking powder
½ - cup chopped walnuts
1 - cup powder sugar - maybe a little more.

Melt chocolate, blend in oil & sugar
add eggs one at a time, beat well after
each addition, add vanilla.
Sift together flour & b. powder; stir into
chocolate mixture, add nuts mix
thoroughly.
Chill dough 2-hours or overnight.
Shape into small balls & roll in powder-
sugar, bake on greased cookie sheet.

Bake 350° - 10-12 min.

The powder sugar coating cracks
apart, giving an interesting effect.

makes 6 dozen 2"cookies

Goodie Bars

1 - box yellow or Chocolate cake mix
½ - cup oil
2 - eggs
1 - cup chocolate chips
½ - cup coconut
½ - cup chopped pecans & walnuts
1 - cup mini marshmallows
Glaze:
1 - T. butter
2 - T. baking cocoa
Powder sugar
hot water

Combine cake mix, oil & eggs. Press into 9"x13" pan.
Sprinkle with chips, nuts & marshmallows

Bake 350° - 25 minutes

Combine glaze ingredients, using - enough sugar & water to make a good drizzling consistency.
Drizzle over baked bars.

Fruit Pizza

1 tube Pillsbury Sugar cookie mix, slice, fit or
Pizza pan, pat together, & bake crust, then –
mix & spread over crust:
8 oz. cream cheese
1/3 cup sugar & 1/2 t. vanilla

Arrange cherries, green grapes, bananas, &
mandarin oranges, in 8" pizza pan.
(Sprinkle bananas with lemon juice)
1 small jar Orange marmalade, thin with
2 t. water, sprinkle this over. Refrigerate.
Bake 250° 12-15 minutes
The crust.

Black Magic Bars

Line jelly roll pan with graham crackers:
Boil: 2 minutes
1 cup butter
1 cup brown sugar) then add
1 cup chopped nuts
Bake 350°   10-15 minutes
last 2 minutes sprinkle with –
Chocolate Chips, when soft spread like
frosting. when cold break in pieces.
nice to put in Christmas boxes.

Graham Pecan Toffy Bars

Line 10"x15" cookie sheet with -
14 graham crackers.

Melt 1/2-lb. margarine in saucepan, add
1 cup brown sugar - bring to boil - boil for
2 minutes, stir constantly - remove
from heat & quickly add 1-t. vanilla &
1-cup chopped pecans, pour over crackers,
spread evenly.   Bake 350° - 10 minutes
Place in refrigerater - when cool, break up.

Toffee Butter Bars

1 - cup butter
1 - cup brown sugar
1 - egg - 1-t. vanilla
2 - cups sifted flour
1 - 6oz. pkg. chocolate chips
1/4 - cup chunky peanut butter
3/4 - cup chopped walnuts
Cream butter, brown sugar, add egg
vanilla, flour - press in 9"x13" pan

Bake 350°   15-20 min.
Melt chocolate chips with peanutbutter - stir until smooth - spread over
cookies, sprinkle with walnuts, cut in
bars.

179

Coconut Cherry Kiss Cookies

½- cup soft butter
1- 3oz. cream cheese - softened
⅔- cup sugar
1- egg yolk
1- t. vanilla & few drops almond extract
1¼- cup flour
2- t. baking powder - ¼-t. salt
½- cup chopped maraschino cherries
5- cups flaked coconut.

Cream butter, sugar & cheese, add egg yolk &
extract. Combine flour, baking powder, salt
add cherries & 3 cups coconut. Chill, make
into 1" balls, roll into additional coconut,
place on ungreased cookie sheet.

Bake 10 mins. 350° oven until
lightly brown.
Press chocolate chip on each.

Lavera Noel

Mrs Field's Cookies

Cream together:
1-lb. butter
2-cups sugar
2- " brown sugar
2- t. Vanilla
4- eggs
mix in another bowl:
4-cups flour
5- " Oatmeal - powdered
1- t. salt
2- t. baking powder
2- t. " soda
add:-to butter mixture
24 oz. Chocolate Chips
1-8oz. Hershey bar grated
3-cups nuts - Optional or white
Chocolate & macadonca nuts
        Bake 375° 6 minutes

makes a lot- freezes well

The secert is the powdered oatmeal
makes them very moist.
Put oatmeal in blender until
   it is powdery. Enjoy.

O'Henry Bars

1 cup sugar
1 cup light corn syrup
1 cup peanut butter
6 cups corn flakes
8 oz. semisweet chocolate chips
8 oz. Butterscotch chips
Cooking spray

Boil sugar & corn syrup in a sauce pan until sugar is dissolved, stirring constantly. Remove from heat & add peanut butter, blending well. Stir in cereal. Press mixture into a 9x13" pan coating with cooking spray.

Melt chocolate & butterscotch chips in microwave until smooth. Spread over cornflake mixture. Cool completely. Cut in Bars.

Rebecca Selzer

German Sugar Cookies

1 - cup water
1½ - cups raisins
1½ - .. sugar
1 - stick butter
2 - t. Vanilla extract
1 - T. coconut ..
3 - eggs
3½ - cups flour
1 - t. baking soda
1 - t. salt

Boil together raisins & water until - almost dry.
Cream sugar, butter, eggs, vanilla and coconut extract. Sift together flour - soda & salt, mix well, add raisins.
Refrigerate overnight.
Form into walnut-size balls, roll in - Sugar.

Bake 350° 10-12 mins.
makes 5 dozen.

This is a soft cookie - freezes well.
I use pam on cookie sheet - they
brown quickly - watch them closely!

Frieda Kofran

very good!

Easy Lemon Bars

1. box one step angel food cake mix
1. 21oz. can lemon pie filling.

With spoon, stir together cake mix &
pie filling - do not use electric mixer.
pour into ungreased jelly roll pan.
Bake 350° 20-25 minutes, cool.
Frost with powder sugar frosting -
flavored with lemon.

Apple or Rhubarb Bars

2. cups flour   ⎫ mix together & press
½. cup sugar   ⎬ in ungreased 10x15" pan
1. " margarine   ⎭ bake 350° 15-20 minutes

Fillings:
4. cups finely chopped fruit
2. " sugar
½. cup flour
4. eggs
Mix ingredients together, pour over
hot crust.
Bake 350° 40-45 minutes
Sprinkle with powder sugar.

Favorite of George

Whirl-A-Way-Cookies

1- cup shortening - oleo, or
1- cup sifted confectioners sugar
2-t. vanilla
1½ - cup sifted flour
1- cup uncooked rolled oats

Cream shortening, add sugar, vanilla,
flour and oats. mix well.
Shape dough into roll & refrigerate,
over night. Cut in slices put on ungreased
cookie sheet.

Sprinkle with colored sugar or
Chocolate sprinkles. Bake 325° - 30 min.

                    Ruth Schmieder

Water Lilies at Amana Lake

185

Mexican Wedding Cookies

½ - cup butter
2 - T. powder sugar
1 - cup flour
1 - cup chopped pecans
1 - t. vanilla

Cream butter & sugar until light.
Add flour, pecans, & Vanilla. Roll -
dough into 1" balls. Place on greased
baking sheet & flatten slightly.
Bake 300° - 25 -30 minutes.
Roll in additional powder sugar -
while warm, let cool, roll again in -
sugar.   25-30 cookies

Be careful to bake only until a
light brown color. Cookies may be
stored for several days with a
light dusting of powder before sering.

                    Alisa M. Emge

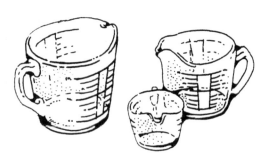

Chocolate Scotcheroos

1-cup sugar   1-cup peanut butter
1-cup light corn syrup
6-cups Rice Krispies

Combine sugar & syrup in 3 qt. saucepan.
Cook over moderate heat, stirring -
frequently, until mixture begins to
bubble. Remove from heat, stir in peanutbutter; mix well. add Rice Krispies, stir
until well blended. Press into buttered
9" x 13" pan.

1-Cup-6oz pkg- Semi-sweet chocolate chips
1-cup "   " Butterscotch - chips.

melt chips together over hot but not
boiling water, stirring until well blended.
Remove from heat, spread evenly over
Rice Krispies mixture - cool until firm.
cut into bars.
          yield: 48 bars 2x1 in.

Duty makes us do things well, but
love makes us do them beautifully.

Cutout Cookies

1. Preheat oven 350°

mix 2 eggs & 1/2 cup of salad oil
With a box of your favorite cake mix
you can add nuts raisins and
chocolate chips to make them special.

Drop dough by teaspoonfull onto a
ungreased cookie sheet spacing 1" apart.
Bake 350° 8-10 minutes

My mothers cut out Cookies

1 1/4 - cup butter   2 - eggs
5 - cups flour   2 - cups sugar
4 - t. baking powder   1 - t. salt
1/2 - cup buttermilk   1 - t. ea. Vanilla & coconut
                                    flavor.
Cream butter, sugar, add eggs.
Sift dry ingredients _ add alternately
with buttermilk, if dough is sticky add
flour to handle. I refrigerate it overnite.
on a floured surface roll out dough -
1/4" thick. cut out with your -
favorite cookie cutter.
Bake on ungreased
cookie sheet -
375° - 8-10 mins.
Do not over bake!

Soft Chocolate Chip Cookies

½ - cup butter
1½ - cups brown sugar
2 - eggs - beaten
2½ - cups flour   sift flour ↵
1 - t. baking soda   b. soda ↵
½ - t. baking powder b. powder together
1 - cup sour cream
1 - 12 oz. chocolate chips

Cream butter & sugar, blend in eggs.
alternately add sifted flour & sour cream,
fold in chocolate chips. Chill - 1 hour.
Drop by t. full on greased cookie sheet.

Bake 350° 10-15 minutes

Elizabeth "Betty" Blechschmidt

Orange Chocolate Truffle Cookies

1- 6oz bag semi-sweet chocolate chips
½- cup sugar
3-T. light corn syrup
½- cup orange juice (can sub. Baileys Irish Cream)
2½- cups crushed vanilla wafer cookies
1- cup chopped pecans or walnuts

Preparation:

Melt chocolate chips in a medium saucepan over
low heat. Stir in ½ cup sugar, corn syrup & juice.
Combine crushed cookies & nuts in a bowl.
Stir in chocolate mixture. Cover and
refrigerate 1 hour, or until firm.
Shape into 1" balls & roll in powder sugar
Store in container at room temperature
1 week before serving.

Makes about 5 dz.

Variation:
Substitute Kahlua or other liquor instead
of juice.
Roll these truffles in powdered unsweetened
cocoa.

Sour Cream Oatmeal Cookies

1½ - cups flour
½ - t. baking soda
1 - cup unsweetend Applesauce
⅓ - " white sugar
½ - " brown sugar
1 egg beaten — 1 t. Vanilla
1 - 6 oz. Chocolate Chips
½ - cup Sour Cream
1½ - cups Oat meal

   Mix applesauce, sugar, egg, Vanill,
add Oatmeal, flour & sour cream, fold
in Chocolate Chips.

   This dough can be made the day
before and stored in refriqerator.

   Bake on greased cookie sheet or
made into bars.

        Bake 350° 10-12 minutes
Can also add coconut or raisins.

Just when a woman thinks her
job is done, she becomes a oma
or (grand mother) But oh what fun!

191

Oatmeal Crispies

Sift:
2-cups flour
1-t. baking soda
½-t   "   powder

Cream:
½-Cup sugar
½-   "   brown sugar
½-   "   margarine
½-   "   unsweetened apple sauce

Add:
1-t. Vanilla
2-eggs well beaten
add:
3-cups quick cook Oatmeal and flour~
1-cup flake coconut or nuts.
mix ~ blend thoroughly.
Drop by teaspoon on greased cookie sheet.

Bake 350° - 10-12 minutes or until
cookies are lightly browned.

Makes 6 dozen.

Oma's Apple Pudding

1½ - cups brown sugar
½ - cup butter or margarine
8 - Apples - peeled & sliced
3 - eggs
1 - cup sugar
4 - T. water
1 - cup flour
1 - t. baking powder
1 - t vanilla

Put brown sugar in greased 8"x 8" baking
dish & dot with butter. (use deep dish)
Place apples on top and cover with batter
made of remaining ingredients.

Bake 350° - 45 minutes - serve warm before
caramel gets hard & sticky.

Serve with ice cream or cream.

This was one of Oma's Selzer's favorite.

Lord Jesus, keep us near You: below You, to learn;
above You, to receive Your support; and beside
You, to be Your friend. Amen.

Rhubarb Crisp

1 - cup sugar
2 - T. flour
⅛ - t. salt
4 - Cups Rhubarb

Mix all ingredients together, put in the bottom of greased 8 x 8" baking dish. Crumble following mixture to cover fruit.

1 - Cup brown sugar
1 - cup oatmeal
1 - cup flour
½ - t. baking powder & ½ - t. baking soda
½ - cup butter softened.

Bake 350° ½ hr or until golden color & fruit cooked.

serve with ice cream

Linda's Bars

1 - box graham Cracker Crumbs
2 - cans Eagle brand Condensed milk
1 - 14 oz. bag of Baker's Coconut
1 - 12 oz. Chocolate Chips - ½ cup nuts

Mix all in a large bowl. Spread in a buttered jelly roll pan. Bake 350° 15-20 minutes. Cool, cut in squares. Dust w/ powered sugar
(toss in bag with sugar)

Very Good!

Honey, Peanutbutter, & Oatmeal Cookies

¾ - cup sugar
¾ - cup honey
¾ - " "super chunk" Peanutbutter

In a large bowl, beat the 3 ingredients
with mixer until creamy.
add - 1 egg
¾ - cup fat free milk
3 - Tablespoons Canola Oil
1 -   "   Vanilla
Combine, in a large bowl
3 - cups (uncooked) Oatmeal
1¾ - " whole wheat flour
1 - teaspoon baking soda
add this to peanutbutter mixture
mix well. Stire in 1 - cup golden
raisins & ½ cup chopped peanuts optional.
Cover & chill 30 minutes or more.
Heat oven 375° Drop rounded T. on
a ungreased cookie sheet.
Bake 8 - 10 minutes. Cool, store in tin
can -   makes 50 or more.
    About 30 calories in one.
    Can sub. Chocolate chips (mini morsels)
in stead of raisins.
Do not overbake. Very good!

194A

Chocolate Cup Cakes

sift
1⅓ - cup flour
1½ - teaspoon Baking powder - dash of salt

Cream - until light + fluffy.
½ - cup butter or margarine
1 - cup sugar

add
3 - eggs (well beaten)
3 - sq. bitter chocolate melted
¾ - cup pecans or walnuts (broken)
¾ - cup raisins
½ - cup milk - 1. teaspoon Vanilla

mix well.
Drop 1 tablespoon into greased cup
cake pan or 1. t. in marquerite pan.
Bake in hot oven 400° 10 min or until
done. Cool. makes 3½ dozen.

Frosting

melt:
2 - squares bitter chocolate (melted)
¼ - cup butter - 1. t. Vanille
3 - 4 cups powder sugar - enough cream
or ½ - ½ to make it nice & smooth
to spread.

I like to freeze the cup cake then
when needed take out, & frost while
still frozen.
I do this with all my cakes.

1948

Oma's Chippy Dippy Bars

1/4 cup melted butter

1 cup Corn flakes crumbs
1 " flaked coconut, packed
1 1/2 cups semi-sweet Chocolate Chips
1 1/2 " Butterscotch Chips
1 cup chopped Walnuts or pecans
14 oz. Can Sweetened condensed milk

Preheat oven 350°
In order given, layer ingredients in
ungreased 9x13 baking pan.
Do not stir.
Bake 28-35 minutes. Depend on oven.
Let cool, cut into 1"-1 1/2" squares

Makes over 3 dozen Bars.

194 C

Chocolate Yummy Bars

1 cup butter or margarine softened
2 cups brown sugar
2 eggs - 2 t. Vanilla
2½ cups sifted flour
1 t. baking soda - 1 t. salt
3 cups quick Oatmeal

In a large bowl, cream butter or margarine with sugar, eggs, & Vanilla. Sift flour, soda & salt, stir in oats, & other ingredients, cream till blended.

Filling —

1 15 oz. can sweetend condensed milk
1 12 oz. pk. Chocolate Chunks (2 cups)
2 T. butter or marg.
2 t. Vanilla - ½ t. salt
1 cup chopped walnuts or pecans,
in a sauce pan, over low heat melt sweet milk, chocolate, butter or marg. stirring till smooth. Stir in Vanilla & nuts.

Pat ⅔ of oat mixture in bottom of greased 10x15x1 inch pan.

Spread chocolate mixture over dough. Dot with remaining oat mixture.

Bake 25-30' at 350° Cool, Cut in 2x1 inch bars. Yields about 75 bars.

Very good
1940

Cherry Bars

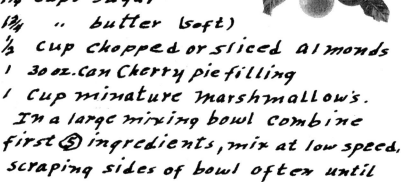

2 cups flour
2 " quick oatmeal
½ t. baking soda
1¼ cups sugar
1¾ " butter (soft)
½ cup chopped or sliced Almonds
1 30 oz. Can Cherry pie filling
1 Cup miniature marshmallow's.
 In a large mixing bowl combine
first ⑤ ingredients, mix at low speed,
scraping sides of bowl often until
crumbly 2-3 minutes, reserve 1½ Cups.
Spread remaining mixture evenly
in 10 x 15 x 1 pan.
 Bake 350° 12 - 15 minutes until brown at
edge. Gently spoon pie filling over
crust & sprinkle with marshmallows
then remaining crumbs. Return to
oven for 25 minutes or until lightly
brown, Cool. Cut in bars.

194 E

Chocolate pudding Cookies

3½ - cups flour — 1 t baking soda
1 - cup butter or margarine softened
½ - cup granulated sugar
½ - cup brown sugar
1 - t. vanilla
1 - pkg. instant chocolate pudding
1 - pkg. 12 oz. chocolate chips
3 - eggs (beaten)
1 - cups chopped walnuts

heat oven to 350°

mix ingredients in order listed.
Drop by teaspoon (full) onto a greased cookie sheet _ bake
12-15 minutes.

I added
½ cup mini chocolate chips
½ " Butterscotch chips
1. " coconut
I omitted _ 12 oz (chocolate chips)
Delicious!

Love is like eating mushrooms,
you're never sure its the real
thing until its too late.

194 F

Toffee Almond Sandies

1 cup butter & 1 cup oil
1 cup sugar & 1 cup powder sugar
1 t. almond extract & 1 t. salt
3½ cups all purpose flour
1 cup whole wheat flour
1 t. baking soda & 1 t. cream of tartar
2 cups chopped almonds
1 pk. English toffee bits

Cream butter & sugar, oil. eggs, extract, mix well.

Combine flour, baking soda, salt and cream of tartar, gradually add to creamed mixture.

Stir in the almonds & toffee bits, shape into ball, roll in sugar flatten with fork.

Bake on ungreased cookie sheet 12-14 minutes until lightly brown.

makes about 12 dozen

Alida Hermann

1946

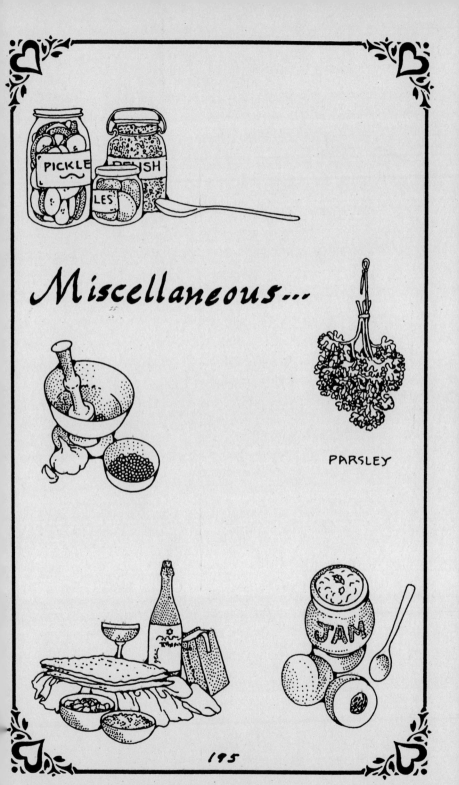

Miscellaneous...

PARSLEY

Caramel Sauce

1-cup firmly packed brown sugar
¼ - " milk
2 - T. butter
1 - t. vanilla

Combine all ingredients in a small saucepan, bring to boil, stir until smooth. Can add sliced bananas if desired or serve separately.

makes 1¼ cup

Fudge Sauce

Combine -
⅓ - cup milk
1 - T. butter

In a saucepan, cook over low heat until butter is melted, add 1-cup Chocolate Chips, stir until melted & smooth, remove from heat stir in ½-t. Vanilla.

Serve warm or cool over ice cream or cake.

makes 1 cup.

Blueberry Sauce

4 - cups blueberries
2 - cups water
1 - cup sugar
1 - T. lemon juice
2 - T. corn starch

Boil first 4 ingredients for 5 minutes
Dissolve cornstarch in ½ cup water
add to boiling berries boil 2-3 min.

Serve over waffles, pancakes or
          rice pudding, ice cream

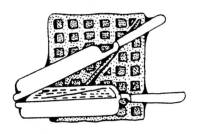

"I need lots of sheer inspiration
plus the guidance to get me there"

Oslo Raisin sauce for Ham

½ - cup golden raisins
½ - " dark "
1½ - cups apple juice
1½ - T. cornstarch
1 - jar.10oz. apple jelly
1 - T. lemon juice

Stir together first 4 ingredients, boil
over low heat, stirring constantly —
until thickened. add apple jelly &
lemon juice — heat until jelly melts.
This makes 2½ cups
            Serve over baked ham.

Gourmet Sauce for Fish

melt ¼ - cup butter, add 2 - T. flour,
stir into a roux.
add 1 - cup chicken stock & ½ cup
light cream — add 1 - T. sherry (optional)
1 - 7oz. can shrimp, chopped to sauce.

        Serve over baked sole
                or other fish

        Serve in gravy boat.

Puppy Chow
"For the two legged one's"

melt
1. stick margarine
1. cup Chocolate Chips
¾. cup peanut butter

Stir in until coated
1-box Crispix

Take a large brown grocery bag, pour
2-cups powder sugar into bag, then
the coated cereal-shake until coated.

Store in airtight container

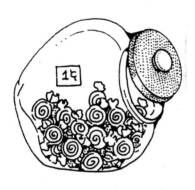

Old Cereal mix

1 - box Rice chex & 1-box wheat chex
½ - box Cherrios
1 - " 4oz. Pretzel sticks
1 lb. mixed nuts
1 - cup butter or margarine
1 - T. garlic salt
1 - T. Onion "
1 - T. Celery "
1 - T. Worcestershire sauce

mix gently & put in open roaster pan.
Bake 2 hours at 200°
Stir occasionally. when cool -
            Store in airtight container

Taco Bowls

Brush each side of a tortilla in room.
temperature oil, place each brushed tortilla
over empty 46oz juice can, place on
baking sheet.
Bake 450° until baked like pie crust.

You can also use a micro safe bowl folding &
shaping the tortilla inside the bowl, then
turn high for 1½ minutes.
The result is a crisp one, lower in calories
and no mess.

Caramel Corn - micro

1 - cup brown sugar
½ - " margarine
¼ - " light corn syrup
½ - t. baking soda
4 - qts. popped corn

Bring sugar, marg. & syrup to a boil 2 min
on high - remove & stir in soda.
Put corn in large brown paper grocery
bag, pour syrup over corn, close bag.
micro 4½ minutes on high. Take
out and shake after each minute —
spread on waxed paper or foil to cool.
Store in airtight container.

The most valuable gift you can give
another is a good example.

Best Popcorn Balls

4 . quarts popped corn
1 . cup light Karo Syrup
½ - .. sugar
1 . t. cream of tartar
1 . T. butter
¼ - t. baking soda

Boil syrup, sugar, & cream of tartar
until a single drop forms a hard ball -
in cold water, then add butter and
soda mix & pour over popcorn & mix.

Put a little butter in your hands, and
form popcorn into balls, be careful
not to burn your hands.

Caramel Corn

2 . cups brown sugar
2 - sticks margarine
½ . cup corn syrup . 1 . t. baking soda
15 - cups popped corn (1½ cup unpopped)
Boil - first 3 ingredients for 5 minutes
Remove from heat add soda, mix quickly.
Pour hot mixture over popped corn,
mix well . bake 200° - 1 hour -
stirring every 15 minutes . When
cool, store in airtight container.

Buttery, Sugary Chex v Nuts Snack

1 - cup butter
½ - " light brown sugar
4 - cups corn Chex
4 - cups rice Chex
4 - cups oat Chex
⅔ - cup filberts
⅔ - cup cashews
⅔ - cup almonds, whole
½ - t. salt

Melt butter in small saucepan v add
sugar. Stir until blended. Place cereal
and nuts in large roasting pan.
Pour butter mixture over top v stir.
Sprinkle on salt v bake 250° in oven -
one hour - stirring mix every 15 min.
Place on paper towels to cool.
Store in air-tight container and -
serve room temp.

Salsa

2 - cups canned tomatoes, undrained &
chopped
1 - medium onion, chopped
2 - cloves of garlic, minced
1 - 4oz. can diced green chilies
½ - t. salt
1 - T. wine vinegar
1 - green pepper, diced
½ - t. chili powder

Mix all ingredients together & cover
leave overnight in refrigerator to blend
flavors.
If finer texture is desired, put
ingredients in blender for few seconds
Versatile salsa may be used as a dip
for corn chips for those who prefer a
mild spicy flavor.

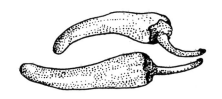

Amana Cheese Spread

1- pound Mun-Chee cheese
1- ¼ inch beer cheese - less then ¼ lb.
1- 12 oz. can Carnation milk - lite

Use large bowl, one you can use in Radarange
Cut cheese in cubes, add ½ of milk - put
in Radarange high for 3 mins. remove
stir with wooden spoon, add more milk
and return to micro for 3 mins - stir
until smooth. When almost done, &
add ½ cup of water.
When done add 1-t. caraway seed
stir well, fill in jars.

The beer cheese gives it zip.

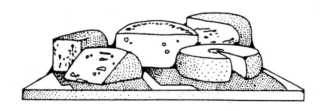

Freezing Sweet Corn

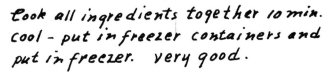

1 - gallon corn   cut off cob.
1 - cup sugar
3 - heaping t. salt
1 - quart water

Cook all ingredients together 10 min.
cool - put in freezer containers and
put in freezer. very good.

Bake Cranberries

1 - pkg. Cranberries - washed v drained - put
berries in large dutch oven pan.
Sprinkle 1/4 cup water v 1/3 cup sugar over
berries - cover with lid.
Bake 325° - 1 hour - check in 1/2 hour - stir
very little, so they do not boil over.
If sugar is not dissolved, bake a little more.

Very good! look like cherries -

Blessed are the meek for
they shall possess the earth.

207

Pickled Beets

2 - quarts beets, prepared as directed
2 - cups sugar
2 - cups vinegar
2 - cups water

Boil beets until tender, drain, let
cold water run over them, peel &
quarter them.
Combine sugar, vinegar, and water
bring to a boil; add beets let come
to boil, fill into sterilized jars & seal.

Green Tomato Pickles

2½ - cups white vinegar

2 - " sugar

¼ - cup dill seed

1 - T. mustard seed

1 - T. celery "

1 - T. pickling salt

5 - lbs. green tomatoes washed & cored

1 - large onion, thinly sliced

In 6-8 qt. saucepot, combine first 6 ingredients, bring to boil. Cut tomatoes into ⅜" thick slices, add tomatoes & onions to syrup. Reduce heat & simmer for 10 minutes, stirring occasionally. Fill hot sterilized jars with tomatoes and hot syrup & seal.

Process in boiling water for 5 minutes

yields 5-6 pints

Pickled Fruit

2 - pounds ground cherries
1 -   "   sugar
4 - oz. vinegar

Mix all ingredients together, boil for
12 -15 minutes fill into sterilized
jars, seal. Store in a cupboard.

Fresh Strawberry Preserves

4 - cups washed hulled strawberries
2 - T. vinegar
3 - cups sugar

Boil berries & vinegar for 3 minutes.
Add sugar stir well. Bring to a rolling boil
and continue boiling - stir often 10-15 min.
Take off heat & skim, let cool, pour into
sterilized jars & seal.

Cucumber Fiskes

2-quarts lg. cucumbers, peeled & sliced-
lengthwise.
½ - cup salt
1½ - cups vinegar
1½ - cups sugar
1½ - cups water
1- head dill

Combine cucumbers & salt, let stand
in earthen crock for 2 hours. Drain.
Bring vinegar, sugar, and water to boil &
pour over cucumbers. add dill. Ready
to serve in 2 days.
Refrigerate, when they are ready.

Tomato Salad

6-tomatoes, skinned and quartered
1-large onion sliced
2-3 T. sugar
2 - T. vinegar
¾-1 - t. salt -Dash of pepper

mix in order given and chill.
Be sure to taste may need more
sugar, vinegar or salt.

Ice Pickles - The Best.

1-gallon unpeeled, washed -sliced cucumbers
3-medium sliced onions
4. cloves garlic
2. peppers - 1 red - 1 green
½ cup salt
1-quart cracked ice

Slice cucumbers ½" thick add onions-
peppers, mix in salt & bury in cracked ice
let stand 3 hours.

Syrup-
5- cups sugar & 3 cups white vinegar
½ - t. turmeric
1½ - t. celery seed
2- T. mustard seed
Boil syrup for 5 minutes, add ½ of
cucumbers (drained) let come to a boil,
put 1 head of dill in clean jar fill with
cucumbers some more dill & 1 clove
garlic on top & fill with syrup & seal.

DILL

Bananas Jamaica

¼ - lb. butter
1 - t. vanilla
6 - T. brown sugar
3 - T. pancake syrup
2 - T. brandy
3 - bananas
Vanilla ice cream

Mix all ingredients except bananas in
shallow sauce pan.
Cook until sugar is dissolved. Add bananas,
turn the bananas until well coated.
Do not over cook.

Serve warm with ice cream.

Rebecca Selzer

213

Grapefruit Wine

You need 1-5 gallon glass (clean) jug - enough
fresh grapefruit that you will have 1 gallon clear
no pulp grapefruit juice.
1 qt. fresh orange or 1 qt. tangerine juice no pulp
has to be clear.
10 lbs sugar

Start with 2 gallons warm water, dissolve
the sugar in it. Pour into jug, add grapefruit
Orange juice, fill jug with water up to 5"- 6"
from top.
Take a piece of clean, white cloth 6"x 6" put
over opening, secure with rubber band, set
in dark place (closet or basement).
Let rest for 8-10 months until it is clear.

It has a beautiful gold
color, and very good!

Tomato Pie

1 - 9" pie crust, unbaked
5 - tomatoes, sliced - salt & pepper to taste
½ - t. oregano
1 - cup chopped green onions-inc. greenstems.
2 - cups grated, sharp Cheddar cheese
1 - cup mayonnaise
½ - " freshly grated Parmesan cheese

Preheat oven 400°. Prick pie crust & bake 10 mins.
remove from oven. Reduce oven to 325°
over   bottom pie crust with 2 layers of tomato
slices. Sprinkle with salt, pepper & ½ of oregano
and onions. Repeat layers.
Combine Cheddar cheese & mayonnaise and
spread over pie. Top with Parmesan.
                    Bake for 45 minutes
                              Serves 6-8

Lord, your gift of prayer can help us turn
fear into faith and despair into hope. Amen.

Baked French Toast

1 - french loaf of bread, cut into 1" slices
6 - eggs (or egg beaters)
1½ - cups half & half or 12 oz. can light evap. skim milk
1 - t. vanilla
¼ - t. cinnamon
¼ - t. nut meg

Lay bread in buttered pan and overlap.
Combine above ingredients - pour over,
cover and refrigerate over nite.

Next day combine:
¼ - cup margarine
½ - " brown sugar
½ - " pecan pieces
1 - T. light corn syrup
Spread over bread.
       Bake 350° - ½ hour, or until
puffed & golden.
       Serve w/maple syrup.

Blueberry sauce would be good too!

Original
No Bake Cookie's

3 - cups quick Oatmeal
½ - Cup Coconut (opt)
½ - Cup Nuts
   mix together

Boil
   2 - Cups Sugar
   ¼ - Cup cocoa
   ½ - " milk
   ½ - " butter

Stir, when its comes to rolling
boil, (time it) Let boil 1½ mins,
take off heat add 3T. peanut
butter - 1 T. vanilla stir well,
pour over oatmeal mixture
mix well until it holds together.
Spoon bite size unto wax paper.
Let cool 2-3 hrs
store in tin Box.

                    Esther Young.

   Also No Bake Bar's on
Page 182 O'Henry Bars
Page 187 Chocolate Scotcheroos

No Bake Cookie's

In a large bowl, mix set aside
3 - cups quick oatmeal
1 - cup Chocolate chips (mini)
½ - cup coconut (opt.)
½ - " nuts

Boil - 2 cups sugar
½ cup milk
½ cup butter

stir, when it comes to a
rolling boil, let boil 1½ mins
take off heat add
2-3 T. peanut butter
¼ - Cup cho Chips
1 - T. vanilla
stir well till creamy
Pour over oatmeal mixture
stir until it holds together,
spoon bite size unto wax paper.
Let rest until dry (2 hrs)
Store in tin box.

Can also use Butterscotch, or
peanut butter chips.

very good!

special

218

Hope we not in this life only,
Christ Himself has made it plain
None who sleep in Him shall perish,
And our faith is not in vain.
Not in vain our glad hosannas;
Since we follow where He led,
Not in vain our Easter anthem:
"Christ has risen from the dead!

A gift for all Occasions
Linda F. Selzer
P. O. Box 96
Homestead, Iowa 52236